Set in Motion

POETS ON POETRY

DAVID LEHMAN, GENERAL EDITOR

A. R. Ammons *Set in Motion*
Douglas Crase *AMERIFIL.TXT*
Suzanne Gardinier *A World That Will Hold All the People*
Kenneth Koch *The Art of Poetry*

DONALD HALL, FOUNDING EDITOR

Martin Lammon, Editor
  Written in Water, Written in Stone
Philip Booth *Trying to Say It*
Joy Harjo *The Spiral of Memory*
Richard Tillinghast
  Robert Lowell's Life and Work
Marianne Boruch *Poetry's Old Air*
Alan Williamson *Eloquence and Mere Life*
Mary Kinzie *The Judge Is Fury*
Thom Gunn *Shelf Life*
Robert Creeley *Tales Out of School*
Fred Chappell *Plow Naked*
Gregory Orr *Richer Entanglements*
Daniel Hoffman *Words to Create a World*
David Lehman *The Line Forms Here*
  · *The Big Question*
Jane Miller *Working Time*
Amy Clampitt *Predecessors, Et Cetera*
Peter Davison
  One of the Dangerous Trades
William Meredith
  Poems Are Hard to Read
Tom Clark *The Poetry Beat*
William Matthews *Curiosities*
Charles Wright *Halflife* · *Quarter Notes*
Weldon Kees
  Reviews and Essays, 1936–55
Tess Gallagher *A Concert of Tenses*
Charles Simic *The Uncertain Certainty*
  · *Wonderful Words, Silent Truth*
  · *The Unemployed Fortune-Teller*
Anne Sexton *No Evil Star*
John Frederick Nims *A Local Habitation*

Donald Justice *Platonic Scripts*
Robert Hayden *Collected Prose*
Hayden Carruth *Effluences from the*
  Sacred Caves · *Suicides and Jazzers*
John Logan *A Ballet for the Ear*
Alicia Ostriker
  Writing Like a Woman
Marvin Bell *Old Snow Just Melting*
James Wright *Collected Prose*
Marge Piercy
  Parti-Colored Blocks for a Quilt
John Haines *Living Off the Country*
Philip Levine *Don't Ask*
Louis Simpson *A Company of Poets*
  · *The Character of the Poet*
  · *Ships Going into the Blue*
Richard Kostelanetz
  The Old Poetries and the New
David Ignatow *Open Between Us*
Robert Francis *Pot Shots at Poetry*
Robert Bly *Talking All Morning*
Diane Wakoski *Toward a New Poetry*
Maxine Kumin *To Make a Prairie*
Donald Davie *Trying to Explain*
William Stafford
  Writing the Australian Crawl ·
  You Must Revise Your Life
Galway Kinnell
  Walking Down the Stairs
Donald Hall *Goatfoot Milktongue*
  Twinbird · *The Weather for Poetry* ·
  Poetry and Ambition · *Death to the*
  Death of Poetry

A. R. Ammons

Set in Motion

ESSAYS, INTERVIEWS,

AND DIALOGUES

Edited by Zofia Burr

Ann Arbor
THE UNIVERSITY OF MICHIGAN PRESS

Copyright © A. R. Ammons 1996
All rights reserved
Published in the United States of America by
The University of Michigan Press
Manufactured in the United States of America
⊚ Printed on acid-free paper

1999 1998 1997 1996   4 3 2 1

A CIP catalog record for this book is available from the British Library.

Library of Congress Cataloging-in-Publication Data

Ammons, A. R., 1926–
    Set in motion : essays, interviews, and dialogues / A. R. Ammons; edited by Zofia Burr.
        p.   cm. —(Poets on poetry)
    ISBN 0-472-09603-6 (alk. paper). —ISBN 0-472-06603-X (pbk. : alk. paper)
    1. Ammons, A. R., 1926– —Interviews.   2. Poets, American —20th century—Interviews.   3. Poetics.   I. Burr, Zofia.
II. Title.   III. Series.
PS3501.M6Z475 1996
811'.54—dc20   96-30225
                                                        CIP

Acknowledgments

I am much obliged to Zofia Burr who brought up the idea of this book, gathered the materials for it, and contributed some of the materials herself. She lent the sustaining spirit for its completion, and her perspicuity and judgment have contributed largely to whatever force the collection has as a whole.

David Lehman has also generously contributed to the text and has brilliantly devised the materials into clarifying parts. I am grateful to him for his warm endorsement of the whole project, as well as for the many late stages of polishing and rearranging he worked through.

Grateful acknowledgment is made to the editors and publishers of the following books, magazines, and newspapers, in which parts of this book originally appeared, sometimes in a different form: *Diacritics; Ommateum with Doxology; Poetry; Epoch; Chelsea; American Poetry Review; Journeywork; North Carolina's 400 Years: Signs Along the Way; Pembroke Magazine; The Best American Poetry 1994; New York Times Book Review; Michigan Quarterly Review; Speak, So I Shall Know Thee: Interviews with Southern Writers; Ecstatic Occasions, Expedient Forms; The Best American Poetry 1988; The Best American Poetry 1989; The Best American Poetry 1990; The Best American Poetry 1993; The Hudson Review;* and *The Yale Review.* Complete citations and publication histories are given on the first page of each piece. Copyright is held by A. R. Ammons. Reprinted with permission of the author. All rights reserved.

Contents

III. Poems and Comment

Editor's Introduction

Since 1955 A. R. Ammons has written over twenty books of poetry. His work has been honored by two National Book Awards, a Guggenheim Fellowship, an American Academy of Arts and Letters Traveling Fellowship, the Levinson Prize, the National Book Critics Circle Award, the Bollingen Prize, an award from the National Institute of Arts and Letters, a Mac-Arthur Prize, and a Lannan Foundation Award. Despite his contribution to contemporary poetry and the public recognition that has been accorded it, Ammons has maintained a certain reticence when it comes to discussing his work. The comments he has made have been scattered across a range of publications and over a long period of time, so that it has been difficult to gather a detailed sense of his own perspective on his works and vocation.

When I suggested that we collect and publish a selection of his prose, Archie was not in favor of the project. The proliferation of prose by poets only seemed to sharpen what he saw as a turning away from the honest complexity of poetic action toward the reductive simplicity of proposition. Only when Ammons saw that the collection could be shaped to articulate the usefulness of poetry to our contemporary situation did he agree to proceed with the project. This book was designed, then, to engage with those who continue to make and read poetry as well as with those inclined to believe that poetry is of no use to us now.

The pieces collected here comprise an attempt to illumi-nate the work of poetry in the contemporary world by way of an extended discussion of Ammons's poetics in particular. The volume has three sections: "Notes," "Interviews," and

"Poems and Comment." The first section consists of short pieces composed between 1955 and 1994. Despite the variety of analogies that Ammons employs to characterize and clarify the work of poetry and despite the sheer span of time that these remarks cover, what is striking is the consistency with which he has formulated his poetics. The second section, four interviews, amplifies Ammons's view of poetry in discussions focused on his poetic process and career. Two of these interviews have not previously been published. The final section includes a selection of Ammons's poetry, along with his remarks on each poem's particular inspiration and effects.

Ammons urges an engagement with poems that is genuinely exploratory. He challenges himself and others—whether we are the poem's maker or its reader—to undertake the poem as a means of casting ahead into something we don't yet understand, rather than using the poem as a means of rediscovering what we think we already know. Because Ammons sees the poem, and the reading of poetry, as a model of *behavior*, he suggests that our basic question about a poem could be, What way of life does this poem seem to be recommending? These writings construe poetry, then, as both exploratory and experimental, and as ethically challenging and committed. They are gathered in this volume in the hope that if we can maintain the ability to be changed by what we encounter in poems, perhaps we can learn to encounter *other people* with the same generosity, and perhaps we can allow these encounters to direct us beyond the limits of our expectations.

I.

Notes

Autobiographical Note

I was born big and jaundiced (and ugly) on February 18, 1926, in a farmhouse four miles southwest of Whiteville, N.C., and two miles northwest of New Hope Elementary School and New Hope Baptist Church. At that time, my sisters were two and six, my father W. M. Ammons thirty-one, and my mother Lucy Della McKee Ammons thirty-eight. My grandfather Randolph had died three years before. My older sister remembers him. One day just before he died, he was sitting on the porch, and he gave her an apple. My grandmother Eliza Williams Ammons was living, but I don't know how old she was. She died when I was eleven. In 1927, I was one. In 1929 a traveling photographer took a picture of me in my navy suit standing in front of the blue hydrangea. I remember that. The next year, my eighteen-month-old brother Elbert died. I remember that. The next year, a brother was born dead. I remember the day of his birth. It was raining hard. My mother screamed and my grandmother walked back and forth crying out with prayer. In 1931 my dog was shot far away from home. He was yellow-brown and came home many times thereafter in my dreams. In 1932 I went to first grade. The next year my big sister fought for me when a cousin said I hadn't done the printing myself. It was beautiful. We had rough times for years. In 1939 I was graduated from New Hope Elementary School. I gave the valedictorian address. In 1943 I was graduated from Whiteville High School. I did not give the valedictorian address. I worked in the shipyard at Wilmington for a while. My boss and I installed fuel pumps on their bases in the

From *Diacritics* 3 (Winter 1973): 2.

bellies of freighters. I went into the navy in 1944, spent some months in the South Pacific, and got out in 1946. I went to Wake Forest College on the GI Bill. My majors were from time to time premed, biology, chemistry, general science. I taught first and married in 1949. I was principal of the three-teacher Hatteras Elementary School, and I married Phyllis Plumbo of Northfield, N.J. My mother died in 1950. By 1952 I had studied English for three semesters at University of California at Berkeley. For twelve years thereafter, I lived in South Jersey where I worked mainly with a glass manufacturing firm. In September 1964 I came to Cornell University. My father died in 1966. My son John Randolph Ammons is seven years old.

Foreword to *Ommateum*

These poems are, for the most part, dramatic presentations of thought and emotion, as in themes of the fear of the loss of identity, the appreciation of transient natural beauty, the conflict between the individual and the group, the chaotic particle in the classical field, the creation of false gods to serve real human needs. While maintaining a perspective from the hub, the poet ventures out in each poem to explore one of the numberless radii of experience. The poems suggest a many-sided view of reality; an adoption of tentative, provisional attitudes, replacing the partial, unified, prejudicial, and rigid; a belief that forms of thought, like physical forms, are, in so far as they resist it, susceptible to change, increasingly costly and violent.

In manner the poems are terse and evocative. They suggest and imply and rather grow in the reader's mind than exhaust themselves in completed, external form. The imagery is generally functional beyond pictoral evocation of mood, as *plateau*, for example, may suggest a flat, human existence, devoid of the drama of rising and falling.

These poems, then, mean to enrich the experience of being; of being anterior to action, that shapes action; of being anterior to wider, richer being.

From A. R. Ammons, *Ommateum with Doxology* (Philadelphia: Dorrance, 1955).

A Note on Prosody

Before, or while, writing a poem, the poet listens to himself as truly as he can to hear how the poem is trying to happen. After the poem is written, he has another chance to listen, not this time to himself but to the poem, to hear what *has* happened. By this unbiased, open listening, the means and use of himself as an instrument are brought more perfectly into knowledge.

I've noticed a few things in my verse lately that arouse my curiosity, and I wonder if they reflect important little real things that are happening to poetry or just willed nerve. Take these few lines:

> and the mountain
> pleased

> but reluctant to
> admit my praise could move it much

> shook a little
> and rained a windrow ring of stones
> to show
> that it was so

Here the box-like structure of rhymed, measured verse is pretty well shot. The emphasis has shifted from the ends of the lines (see German sentence structure, see the concluding emphasis that rhyme itself imposes) toward the left-hand margin. A slightly stronger than usual emphasis is given to *and: mountain* is played down, aided by its feminine ending: *pleased,*

From *Poetry* 203, no. 3 (June 1963): 202–3.

being one sound, has no beginning or end: *to* / *admit* fractures the movement so that an artificial emphasis is given to *to* but only so that even more weight can fall with *admit* at the beginning of the line: *much* ends the line emphatically, but after all both lines are suspended between *pleased* and *shook,* so that all the weight actually falls at the beginning of a line again. The last three lines have the emphasis at the end, though *that* in the last line receives more than normal stress.

What I think is illustrated by so tiny a fragment of verse is that both ends are being played against a middle. The center of gravity is an imaginary point existing between the two points of beginning and end, so that a downward pull is created that gives a certain downward rush to the movement, something like a waterfall glancing in turn off opposite sides of the canyon, something like the right and left turns of a river.

The caesura of traditional verse, the fact that it was consciously, magnificently employed, may suggest that it acted as a counterweight to the heavy-ended couplets, that it was a correction of the center of gravity, so that the lines would be poised in balance, instead of slanting down to heavy stops. Of course, the caesura could not balance the line: that would have destroyed the couplet effect. But it could echo the line-end and so shift some of the weight to the left.

A central poise suggests the pendulum: it is held in an instant of sight at either extremity of its swing, but what it is constantly operating around is the bottom point of its downward swing. Though there is an emphasis of light and "stillness" at either extremity, the real center is passed in rapid motion.

I think the quoted fragment and these thoughts suggest that a nonlinear movement is possible which uses both the beginning and the end of the line as glancing-off points, so that the movement is not across the page but actually, centrally down the page.

A Note on Incongruence

Another trial definition: a poem is a linguistic correction of disorder. A thing, made of language, a system of signs, symbols, pictures, is created which is consistently itself.

So, poetry is not made out of "reality" but out of an invented system of signs. Then, where does the disorder come from? Is it a linguistic disorder linguistically corrected? Is poetry a purification or policing of language?

What is the nature of the disorder? Hundreds of thousands of words are listed in the dictionary with merely alphabetical connection. We combine a few words into a phrase; then, more words into a clause, sentence, paragraph, chapter, novel. Meaning (or the revelation of meaninglessness) ideally becomes denser and more complete as the mass of definition grows. The whole novel engages more experience and gives it greater accuracy of communication than a sentence or a paragraph can. Multiplicity is accumulated into symmetry. Shape is given.

But where is the disorder? Not in the dictionary—that is not the disorder but quantity, a mass of fragments, elements that in certain configurations can convey meaning.

How does the system of language connect with what it points to? Obviously, the language, an invented instrument, is not identical with what it points to, although it is one of the best ways of pointing we have. What is pointed at may or may not be disorderly. It would be presumptuous to call "reality" disorderly, since our calling can be done only in terms of language.

From *Epoch* 15 (Winter 1966): 192.

Try again, then. Where does the disorder come from? What is being reconciled in a poem or novel or play?

The disorder may be sensed as an incongruence between our nonverbal experience of reality and our language reflection of it.

If feeling is an essence that results from the mind's effort to make innumerable sensuous events apprehendable (capable of being acted on), then it may be that as our conscious attention brings more and different events (facts) before the mind, and as these events settle into the unconscious and return as "feelings," we begin to sense a disjointure between our feelings and our linguistic expression of them.

At that point, a new poem becomes necessary. That is, a language system needs to be created which does ampler justice to the facts behind the feelings. A closer congruence needs to be achieved between the reality and the reflection.

Facts change or new facts accumulate, disturbing the habitual response. The mind seeks the new object that can adequately reflect and interpret the new feelings. Disorder becomes incongruence and the poem is a *linguistic* correction to congruence. The facts may stay the same or go on changing, but we are temporarily able to cope.

Note of Intent

A couple of years ago, shortly after a review by Wendell Berry of one of my books appeared in the *Nation*[1]—a review in which Mr. Berry noted my use in some poems of scientific terminology—Sonia Raiziss[2] wrote to me suggesting that I edit an issue of *Chelsea* to contain poems having to do with science and technology.

I agreed to do this and Miss Raiziss and I began to notify poets we could contact by letter of our intention. To help us reach poets we did not already know, Henry Rago carried a notice of our plan in *Poetry*.

Obviously, the intention—poems having to do with science and technology—is so broad as to lack all useful definition. We felt, though, that only a broad definition could serve our purpose, which was exploratory, and which was to discover definition, if any were possible, from the poems themselves: that is, we felt that easy, a priori definition should give place to the rich, self-contradicting, complex "world" to be outlined by the hoped-for poems themselves.

Since I alone was to select the poems, however, a heavy restraint had to be acknowledged: my predispositions, limitations, blind spots would interfere with any world that was trying to become itself, to reach toward a complicated definition. I probably did not succeed in ridding myself of the inappropriate self entirely. After all, no part of the self is

---

From *Chelsea* 20/21 (May 1967): 3–4.

1. Review of *Expressions of Sea Level, Nation* 198: 304 (March 23, 1964).

2. Editor of *Chelsea* at the time this was written.

inappropriate to part of the task—the question. Is this a poem?

Consciously, then, I tried to keep my mind open to all possibility, to alarm myself at the encroachment of an idiosyncrasy. But since it is at least as difficult to know oneself as to talk about the relations between poetry and science, I have undoubtedly exercised, if unconsciously, some control on the world presented by these poems.

I did use one governing assumption: that it doesn't matter what a poem is about unless it succeeds first in being a poem. In other words, in spite of the fact that we have devoted an issue to science and technology, we have felt that these provide "materials" for poems but that poems themselves are primary. I think it is legitimate to maintain this order and still focus attention on the experience resulting from contact with scientific materials. Much of what is impersonally, flatly new to us arises from scientific insight and technological innovation. It is part of the result of a poem to personalize and familiarize, to ingest and acquaint—to bring feelings and things into manageable relationships.

In this connection, Wordsworth's statement in the *Preface*[3] has been my guide and shelter:

> If the time should ever come when what is now called Science, thus familiarized to men, shall be ready to put on, as it were, a form of flesh and blood, the Poet will lend his divine spirit to aid the transfiguration, and will welcome the Being thus produced, as a dear and genuine inmate of the household of man.

Here, then, are poems—properly, not all welcoming—that give us the best knowledge that could be managed under the circumstances of the relation between poetry and science in our time. Each reader will come away with a different experience of this knowledge, but possibly the experiences of readers will be more nearly alike than unlike.

---

3. Ammons is referring to the "Preface to *Lyrical Ballads*," 1802.

A Poem Is a Walk

Nothing that can be said
in words is worth saying.

—Lao-tse

I don't know whether I can sustain myself for thirty minutes of saying I know nothing—or that I need to try, since I might prove no more than you already suspect, or, even worse, persuade you of the fact. Nothingness contains no images to focus and brighten the mind, no contrarieties to build up muscular tension: it has no place for argumentation and persuasion, comparison and contrast, classification, analysis. As nothingness is more perfectly realized, there is increasingly less (if that isn't contradictory) to realize, less to say, less need to say. Only silence perfects silence. Only nothingness contributes to nothingness. The only perfect paper I could give you would be by standing silent before you for thirty minutes. But I am going to try this imperfect, wordy means to suggest why silence is finally the only perfect statement.

I have gone in for the large scope with no intention but to make it larger; so I have had to leave a lot of space "unworked," have had to leave out points the definition of any one of which could occupy a paper longer than this. For though we often need to be restored to the small, concrete, limited, and certain, we as often need to be reminded of the large, vague, unlimited, unknown.

I can't tell you where a poem comes from, what it is, or

From *Epoch* 18 (Fall 1968): 114–19. Delivered to the International Poetry Forum in Pittsburgh in April 1967.

what it is for: nor can any other man. The reason I can't tell you is that the purpose of a poem is to go past telling, to be recognized by burning.

I don't, though, disparage efforts to say what poetry is and is for. I am grateful for—though I can't keep up with—the flood of articles, theses, and textbooks that mean to share insight concerning the nature of poetry. Probably all the attention to poetry results in some value, though the attention is more often directed to lesser than to greater values.

Once every five hundred years or so, a summary statement about poetry comes along that we can't imagine ourselves living without. The greatest statement in our language is Coleridge's in the *Biographia*. It serves my purpose to quote only a fragment from the central statement: that the imagination—and, I think, poetry—"reveals itself in the balance or reconciliation of opposite or discordant qualities." This suggests to me that description, logic, and hypothesis, reaching toward higher and higher levels of generality, come finally to an antithesis logic can't bridge. But poetry, the imagination, can create a vehicle, at once concrete and universal, one and many, similar and diverse, that is capable of bridging the duality and of bringing us the experience of a "real" world that is also a reconciled, a unified, real world. And this vehicle is the only expression of language, of words, that I know of that contradicts my quotation from Lao-tse, because a poem becomes, like reality, an existence about which nothing that can be said in words is worth saying.

Statement can also achieve unity, though without the internal suspension of variety. For example, All is One, seems to encompass or erase all contradiction. A statement, however, differs from a work of art. The statement, All is One, provides us no experience of manyness, of the concrete world from which the statement derived. But a work of art creates a world of both one and many, a world of definition and indefinition. Why should we be surprised that the work of art, which overreaches and reconciles logical paradox, is inaccessible to the methods of logical exposition? A world comes into being about which any statement, however revelatory, is a lessening.

Knowledge of poetry, which is gained, as in science or other areas, by induction and deduction, is likely to remain provisional by falling short in one of two ways: either it is too specific, too narrow and definite, to be widely applicable—that is, the principles suggested by a single poem are not likely to apply in the same number or kind in another poem: or, the knowledge is too general, too abstract and speculative, to fit precisely the potentialities of any given poem. Each poem in becoming generates the laws by which it is generated: extensions of the laws to other poems never completely take. But a poem generated by its own laws may be unrealized and bad in terms of so-called objective principles of taste, judgment, deduction. We are obliged both to begin internally with a given poem and work toward generalization *and* to approach the poem externally to test it with a set—and never quite the same set—of a priori generalizations. Whatever we gain in terms of the existence of an individual poem, we lose in terms of a consistent generality, a tradition: and vice versa. It is Scylla and Charybdis again. It is the logically insoluble problem of one and many.

To avoid the uncertainty generated by this logical impasse—and to feel assured of something definite to teach—we are likely to prefer one side or the other—either the individual poem or the set of generalizations—and then to raise mere preference to eternal verity. But finally, nothing is to be gained by dividing the problem. A teacher once told me that every line of verse ought to begin with a capital letter. That is definite, teachable, mistaken knowledge. Only by accepting the uncertainty of the whole can we free ourselves to the reconciliation that is the poem, both at the subconscious level of feeling and the conscious level of art.

One step further before we get to the main business of the paper. Questions structure and, so, to some extent predetermine answers. If we ask a vague question, such as, What is poetry? we expect a vague answer, such as, Poetry is the music of words, or Poetry is the linguistic correction of disorder. If we ask a narrower question, such as, What is a conceit? we are likely to get a host of answers, but narrower answers. Proteus is a good figure for this. You remember that Proteus was a minor sea god, a god of *knowledge,* an attendant on Poseidon.

Poseidon is the ocean, the total view, every structure in the ocean as well as the unstructured ocean itself. Proteus, the god of knowledge, though, is a minor god. Definite knowledge, knowledge specific and clear enough to be recognizable as knowledge, is, as we have seen, already limited into a minor view. Burke said that a clear idea is another name for a little idea. It was presumed that Proteus knew the answers—and more important The Answer—but he resisted questions by transforming himself from one creature or substance into another. The more specific, the more binding the question, the more vigorously he wrestled to be free of it. Specific questions about poetry merely turn into other specific questions about poetry. But the vague question is answered by the ocean which provides distinction and nondistinction, something intellect can grasp, compare, and structure, and something it can neither grasp, compare, nor structure.

My predisposition, which I hope shortly to justify, is to prefer confusion to oversimplified clarity, meaninglessness to neat, precise meaning, uselessness to overdirected usefulness. I do not believe that rationality can exhaust the poem, that any scheme of explanation can adequately reflect the poem, that any invented structure of symbology can exceed and thereby replace the poem.

I must stress here the point that I appreciate clarity, order, meaning, structure, rationality: they are necessary to whatever provisional stability we have, and they can be the agents of gradual and successful change. And the rational, critical mind is essential to making poems: it protects the real poem (which is nonrational) from blunders, misconceptions, incompetences; it weeds out the second rate. Definition, rationality, and structure are ways of seeing, but they become prisons when they blank out other ways of seeing. If we remain open-minded we will soon find for any easy clarity an equal and opposite, so that the sum of our clarities should return us where we belong, to confusion and, hopefully, to more complicated and better assessments.

Unlike the logical structure, the poem is an existence which can incorporate contradictions, inconsistencies, explanations and counter-explanations and still remain whole, unexhausted and inexhaustible; an existence that comes about by means other than those of description and exposition and, therefore, to be met by means other than, or in addition to, those of description and exposition.

With the hope of focusing some of these problems, I want now to establish a reasonably secure identity between a poem and a walk and to ask how a walk occurs, what it is, and what it is for. I say I want a reasonably secure identity because I expect to have space to explore only four resemblances between poems and walks and no space at all for the differences, taking it for granted that walks and poems are different things. I'm not, of course, interested in walks as such but in clarification or intensification by distraction, seeing one thing better by looking at something else. We want to see the poem.

What justification is there for comparing a poem with a walk rather than with something else? I take the walk to be the externalization of an interior seeking, so that the analogy is first of all between the external and the internal. Poets not only do a lot of walking but talk about it in their poems: "I wandered lonely as a cloud," "Now I out walking," and "Out walking in the frozen swamp one grey day." There are countless examples, and many of them suggest that both the real and the fictive walk are externalizations of an inward seeking. The walk magnified is the journey, and probably no figure has been used more often than the journey for both the structure and concern of an interior seeking.

How does a poem resemble a walk? First, each makes use of the whole body, involvement is total, both mind and body. You can't take a walk without feet and legs, without a circulatory system, a guidance and coordinating system, without eyes, ears, desire, will, need: the total person. This observation is important not only for what it includes but for what it rules out: as with a walk, a poem is not simply a mental activity: it has body, rhythm, feeling, sound, and mind, conscious and subconscious. The pace at which a poet walks (and thinks), his natural breath-length, the line he pursues, whether forthright and straight or weaving and meditative, his whole "air," whether of aimlessness or purpose—all these things and many more figure into the "physiology" of the poem he writes.

A second resemblance is that every walk is unreproducible, as is every poem. Even if you walk exactly the same route each time—as with a sonnet—the events along the route cannot be imagined to be the same from day to day, as the poet's health, sight, his anticipations, moods, fears, thoughts cannot be the same. There are no two identical sonnets or villanelles. If there were, we would not know how to keep the extra one: it would have no separate existence. If a poem is each time new, then it is necessarily an act of discovery, a chance taken, a chance that may lead to fulfillment or disaster. The poet exposes himself to the risk. All that has been said about poetry, all that he has learned about poetry, is only a partial assurance.

The third resemblance between a poem and a walk is that each turns, one or more times, and eventually *re*turns. It's conceivable that a poem could take out and go through incident after incident without ever returning, merely ending in the poet's return to dust. But most poems and most walks return. I have already quoted the first line from Frost's "The Wood-Pile." Now, here are the first three lines:

> Out walking in the frozen swamp one gray day,
> I paused and said, 'I will turn back from here.
> No, I will go on farther—and we shall see.'

The poet is moving outward seeking the point from which he will turn back. In "The Wood-Pile" there is no return: return is implied. The poet goes farther and farther into the swamp until he finds by accident the point of illumination with which he closes the poem.

But the turns and returns or implied returns give shape to the walk and to the poem. With the first step, the number of shapes the walk might take is infinite, but then the walk begins to "define" itself as it goes along, though freedom remains total with each step: any tempting side road can be turned into on impulse, or any wild patch of woods can be explored. The pattern of the walk is to come true, is to be recognized, discovered. The pattern, when discovered, may be found to apply to the whole walk, or only a segment of the walk may prove to have contour and therefore suggestion and shape.

From previous knowledge of the terrain, inner and outer, the poet may have before the walk an inkling of a possible contour. Taking the walk would then be searching out or confirming, giving actuality to, a previous intuition.

The fourth resemblance has to do with the motion common to poems and walks. The motion may be lumbering, clipped, wavering, tripping, mechanical, dance-like, awkward, staggering, slow, etc. But the motion occurs only in the body of the walker or in the body of the words. It can't be extracted and contemplated. It is nonreproducible and nonlogical. It can't be translated into another body. There is only one way to know it and that is to enter into it.

To summarize, a walk involves the whole person; it is not reproducible: its shape occurs, unfolds: it has a motion characteristic of the walker.

If you were brought into a classroom and asked to teach walks, what would you teach? If you have any idea, I hope the following suggestions will deprive you of it.

The first thought that would occur to you is, What have other people said about walks? You could collect all historical references to walks and all descriptions of walks, find out the average length of walks, through what kind of terrain they have most often proceeded, what kind of people have enjoyed walks and why, and how walks have reflected the societies in which they occurred. In short, you could write a history of walks.

Or you could call in specialists. You might find a description of a particularly disturbing or interesting walk and then you might call in a botanist to retrace that walk with you and identify all the leaves and berries for you: or you might take along a sociologist to point out to you that the olive trees mentioned were at the root—forgive me—of feudal society: or you might take along a surveyor to give you a close reading in inches and degrees: or you might take a psychoanalyst along to ask good questions about what is the matter with people who take walks: or you might take a physiologist to provide you with astonishment that people can walk at all. Each specialist would no doubt come up with important facts and insights, but your attention, focused on the cell structure of the olive leaf, would miss the main event, the walk itself.

You could ask what walks are good for. Here you would find plenty: to settle the nerves, to improve the circulation, to break in a new pair of shoes, to exercise the muscles, to aid digestion, to prevent heart attacks, to focus the mind, to distract the mind, to get a loaf of bread, to watch birds, to kick stones, to spy on a neighbor's wife, to dream. My point is clear. You could go on indefinitely. Out of desperation and exasperation brought on by the failure to define the central use or to exhaust the list of uses of walks, you would surrender, only to recover into victory by saying, Walks are useless. So are poems.

Or you could find out what walks mean: do they mean a lot of men have unbearable wives, or that we must by outward and inward motions rehearse the expansion, and contraction of the universe; do walks mean that we need structure—or, at an obsessive level, ritual in our lives? The answer is that a walk doesn't mean anything, which is a way of saying that to some extent it means anything you can make it mean—and always more than you can make it mean. Walks are meaningless. So are poems.

There is no ideal walk, then, though I haven't taken the time to prove it out completely, except the useless, meaningless walk. Only uselessness is empty enough for the presence of so many uses, and only through uselessness can the ideal walk come into the sum total of its uses. Only uselessness can allow the walk to be totally itself.

I hope you are now, if you were not before, ready to agree with me that the greatest wrong that can be done a poem is to substitute a known part for an unknown whole and that the choice to be made is the freedom of nothingness: that our experience of poetry is least injured when we accept it as useless, meaningless, and nonrational.

Besides the actual reading in class of many poems, I would suggest you do two things: first, while teaching everything you can and keeping free of it, teach that poetry is a mode of discourse that differs from logical exposition. It is the mode I spoke of earlier than can reconcile opposites into a "real" world both concrete and universal. Teach that. Teach the distinction.

Second, I would suggest you teach that poetry leads us to the unstructured sources of our beings, to the unknown, and returns us to our rational, structured selves refreshed. Having once experienced the mystery, plenitude, contradiction, and composure of a work of art, we afterward have a built-in resistance to the slogans and propaganda of oversimplification that have often contributed to the destruction of human life. Poetry is a verbal means to a nonverbal source. It is a motion to no-motion, to the still point of contemplation and deep realization. Its knowledges are all negative and, therefore, more positive than any knowledge. Nothing that can be said about it in words is worth saying.

Surfaces

Writing poetry is like surfing. The surfboard is the technique, the mastered means by which one is enabled to participate in the energy, greater than one's own energy, of the waves. The ecstasy of coordination between the mind, body, the surfboard, and the surf reaches its highest intensity in what is called "shooting the curl"—that is, the finding of near immobility in motion, the finding the groove where with least surfboard action one "dwells" in the ongoing, onbreaking wave. The bringing of all the forces into this momentary symmetry of actions allows one to participate in an apparently easy, effortless harmony of things.

There are waves in the self, as we all know, moments of such consonance between the body, the will, the wish, the intellect that we lose consciousness of any elements of disharmony and feel that our own expressiveness is inseparable from all expressiveness. When a wave of some size arises in us, we are not exactly swept away, but we do thrash out with our surfboard, stand up for the subtlest steering, and try to catch the wave. If we miss or if the wave isn't right or fulfilling—that is, if the wave is not a whole motion of unfolding, an integrated action—we spill, and the poem ends in the confusion of grinding bottom, the surfboard tossed free and wild, the self made the object of, rather than the master of, forces greater than itself.

But if the wave is right and we are right, if our attention and concentration and technique are perfect, we experience one of the ardent and supreme moments of our lives, the

From *American Poetry Review* (July/August 1974): 53.

maximum liveliness with the maximum symmetry. It is the delight that this is in itself that surfers and poets want to touch, to know, a delight that is knowledge, since the experience is of an order never to be forgotten, a knowledge of an alignment open to us.

Fine for the poet or surfer who can do this. But what about us. What if we are not able or are no longer able to surf but want to "enter in," to know how it feels? How can we learn? We watch carefully, we note the various theories and styles of surfing, we learn the technique, too, so we can savor the difference between the masterful or clumsy use of it, the innovative or serendipitous use of it, we contemplate the action till we seem to dwell in it, we come to exist in the action with almost as much, if not as much, maybe as much, certainty of knowledge, trueness of being, as the surfer feels.

We may want, having felt the magic, to know which surfer learned from which surfer, how the surfboard took on through history the particular dynamics of its shape, where the best beaches are, what kinds of waves are capable of producing what kinds of action, etc. There is much to be known, an endless amount, and all of it adds to, but is for, the feeling.

But what we know and feel prepares us only partly for the next wave. It will be a new wave, it will be entered into at a slightly different crest, it will unwind according to its own specific tensions and releases, it will be a new possibility in the specific, however much it will resemble previous specifics. Poetry, like surfing, is inexhaustibly fresh and surprising, its delights are endless, and each wave, like each poem, contributes its measure to what we feel, know, and believe.

Differences of Degree

Concerning literary matters, we can differentiate and define ourselves as either entanglers or untanglers. The entanglers reach out for a synthesis made up of strands of rhythm, streaks of images, textures of sound, tones, colors, fragments transmuted into the winding assimilations of knots, dispositions into design, leading to the emergence of a new "thing," an inexhaustible presence imitating life. Untanglers come on such formations and show how the organizing principle of the "thing" found its disposition, how the disposition resembles others of its kind, what the disposition might mean, or what development might be discerned through a history of similar dispositions. Entanglers and untanglers represent two of the most noticeable forms of intellectual procedure in English departments today. Today, because although the two forms of mind date back as far as texts go, only recently with the appearance of writers in English departments has the differentiation become operative.

We all use both forms of procedure, of course. Poets weigh the justness of their imaginative actions with as much nicety as critics define a point. And critics form their discursiveness into dispositions as carefully as poets articulate structures. But wherever a difference, so clear and coherent, can force a division, it usually does. That it might occasion an incorporative broadening is less often noticed or attempted.

The entanglers appeal to actions, dispositions, syntheses, auras, silences, while the untanglers seek disclosure, exposition,

From *Journeywork* 1 (Fall 1984).

analysis, anatomy, announcement, followed usually by reconstructive syntheses of their own. Why should we not allow and encourage, if only in our departments, a full representation of the human possibility? Why must we defer so much to easy differentiation when we might have before us the richness and possibility of a more nearly inclusive scope?

This anthology demonstrates that power of mind belongs as much to the entanglers as to others. It may be that literary criticism is the real poetry of our time or, more, that real poetry is a poetry of concept and statement, not of body and stillness. But wherever the poiesis comes from, it is there we look to find the vitalizing propositions. Why not let all of us who work with language follow our inclinations, entangling or untangling, or both, and let those who speak to us most acutely be our speakers? That would give English departments the responsibility to uphold excellence and scope, and it would give us the chance to grow into the abundance possible to sharing, rather than to restrict us into the narrowing extreme of a single kind of mental activity. Scholarship and criticism support the definitions we now promote as epistemology, but there is more than one kind of knowing. Our writing programs around the country are doing their part to make differences the groundwork of larger forms.

Taking Exception

I guess an interesting question, not answerable in brief, is how does a regular person become a poet? Where does she acquire the platform or stance or calling that enables her to speak, and how does her assuming the platform affect her community, state, or nation? In that question alone are many subsidiary questions, several times more questions than there are poets, and even more answers. But one question can serve as an axis to wind some thoughts around.

What happens when a citizen takes exception to something? She defines herself in some degree away from an image of herself or her world agreed on by the community as the proper image. For example, a mother could take exception to the mother image society identifies her by. She could protest that the image, unacknowledged and automatic, is a form of tyranny not arising from nature, as it may sometimes seem, but a definition and imposition arrived at by the dynamics of the culture. The mother surprises in herself much energy not expressed by the mother image: she may want to serve others but not always serve others; she may be interested in carpentry or in business administration; she may wish to think of herself as a human equal, having access to equal rights and equal pay.

The part of her potential nature that society's imposed image excludes from her own definition of herself becomes the exception she takes, the break, the halt, the inward hesitation

From the Introduction to *North Carolina's 400 Years: Signs Along the Way*, edited by Ronald H. Bayes (Durham, N.C.: Acorn Press, 1986), vii–viii.

that must erupt into speech. This is the platform, I think. This is the vocation, the calling. And this is where what poets say begins a complicated relationship with what societies are. The poet from the humble separation of her platform declares a difference with society, a difference brought on by an over-looked wrong to the fullest possibility of her nature. Society, operating most smoothly when most homogeneous, resents the disturbance of a difference and marginalizes the poet, attempting to re-right itself by stamping out the difference. But the poet knows that growth and change tremble in and out of focus where lives are on the line, the poet's lines them-selves cutting out a difference on the page that imitates the introduction of the difference into the world. If the an-nounced difference stirs, redefines, completes others, a ten-dency develops in the society that may sweep away into a new time.

The poet finds some part of her identity excluded from becoming operational in society. She notes that exclusion in herself, takes exception to thinking of herself in that way, mounts the platform of the exception, and administers the disturbances, the painful rifts of context that may eventually bring better things.

But helpful, necessary as it is for poets to sense shifts in tone and meaning in their worlds, to call attention to them and take exception to them, it is essential for larger purposes that the poet do all this with astonishing competence, with visionary authority. If the poet only notes and cures ills in her own time, she is locked in that time (or space or region) and becomes irrelevant as soon as the issue she has addressed is no longer an issue. But if the making of the poem, the coordina-tion of word, image, rhythm is deeply moving, if the land-scape of the mind presented is overwhelmingly enchanting, the poem takes on a value in itself, just as a basketball game beautifully played is meaningful beyond winning and losing, though winning and losing, as in wars and as any Southerner knows, is extremely important.

The chief point I want to make has to do with the energies poets feel and cause with their local concerns and what can happen more broadly because of those energies. Local, regional concerns may bring poets to life as they address wrongs and rights, but if a poet happens also to address the wrongs and rights with commanding beauty, she becomes of interest not only to her own community and region but to the whole country and, conceivably, to the whole world.

I've tried to draw a big curve, meanwhile protesting that it's impossible to draw such curves justly and quickly. The poet takes exception to the way things are. The difference she notes becomes her minority platform. The minority status, the lack of endorsement, of the platform presses anger and risk into the arrogance of speech. The speech finds resonance, or doesn't, in the society, and the poet witnessing agreeable change gratefully accepts the honors society gratefully bestows on her. But if the speech was beautiful, many other causes and countries will be attracted in order to praise what was beautifully achieved.

So many poems in the anthology following present the liveliness I have been trying to name. In Lenard Moore's poem, the unfamiliar keeps arising within the familiar; the will to rebellion is quietly represented in Helen Goodman's "Edenton Tea Party"; I am deeply touched by the exactness of place, the love and rage of Elizabeth Bolton's poem; the graphic realism of Shelby Stephenson's language releases us from the temptations of sentimentality; Lu Overton, Evolyn Rinehart, Mary Kratt, and so many others bring the perceptions and feelings of poets to the rest of us, so much so as to tell us that North Carolina is a homeland of its own where the language is used in a way to interest everybody.

A Paragraph of Precedence

The work of art is undertaken by the practitioner as a means of finding out and defining (if just tonally) something he doesn't already know. The elaboration of known or imaginable positions in morality, epistemology, politics, feminism needs no forms not already available to rationality and produces no surprise. In art, the form enables a self-becoming that brings up in its arising materials not previously touched on or, possibly, suspected. This confers the edge of advancement we call creativity. The work of art in its primary thrust must be uncompromised by utilitarian aims or applications of any kind so as to prevent all hindrance to the emergences of its newness as a thing-in-itself. Any use, provided standing ideologies allow, can then be made of the work.

From *Pembroke Magazine* 18 (1986).

Poetry Is Action

Language is the medium that carries the inscription, but what is inscribed in poetry is action, not language. The body of the ice-skater is only the means to an inscription on ice. Beautiful as the body may be, the inscription does not exist for the purpose of the body but of what the body does, what its doings symbolize.

Magnificently great about poetry is that its action is like other actions. It stands not as an isolated, esoteric activity but as a formal and substantive essentializing of all action. The ice-skater cuts formal figures in which the precision of execution is a high value, or she emerges clownish on the ice and imitates the hilarious sloppy falls we all sometimes commit; the invention of free style is always instantaneous, however many years of practice are in evidence. She engages the tensions we seek that relate our moments to our stories; though she is at any given second only *there,* she writes in our minds the full disclosure of the action which we afterward, perhaps ever after, contemplate as a source and model of what dynamics might be and what values they might emphasize.

So poetry for me is a symbolic action shown by language and revealing what we would have our behavior imitate or strive for. This is perhaps least of all to imply good behavior. It is often, as in ice-skating contests, a drive toward competition, dominance, and victory over others. It can be ruthless, as

From the Introduction to *The Best American Poetry 1994,* edited by A. R. Ammons; series editor, David Lehman (New York: Scribners, 1994).

ruthless in its perhaps deceptive and small way as a Caesar or Khan in his great way.

Poets of unconventional appearance and behavior are in some periods greatly exposed to danger. An unconventional sexual proclivity, for example, can induce hatred to the point of murder. To thrive in such a world, the poet must disguise himself so as to live efficiently enough with others to risk revealing himself. Insects' bodies imitate twigs and leaves so as to be present but invisible to their predators. When they are most visible, flashing bright oranges and reds, their gambit is to advertise openly that they are poisonous if eaten. Poets are sometimes glaringly unconventional and so are openly ostracized, but even the hostile enforcers of social codes may want, half-willingly, to be free, as free as the artist they profess to despise. Poets deceive to protect themselves; they may need to transform their strategies before they take the sometimes heavy chance of bringing forward a work of true originality. History is full of this, of this most of all.

Poetry is not innocent, not sweet, not just sweet. It charms to convince, deceive, make room, find a way to autonomy and freedom. We owe to those who deal at the center of these dynamics the vitality of our lives.

In recent years literary criticism has greatly enriched itself by strong solicitations of the poem. I suppose we should all be grateful for the critical positionings that have permitted us to look anew at our fundamental estimates of what poems are or can be. I think no one would choose to go on indefinitely with unalterable programs touching our use of words. Even if we ultimately settle for a slight change of perspective when we had at first supposed a revolution of values was upon us, we are likely to be grateful for both the initial pleasant disturbance and the bit of freshness detectable in the aftermath.

So I for one—and this is one time I assume majorities agree with me—am delighted with the stir that has lately surrounded the art, especially the literary art, scene. My knowledge of the origin and nature of recent theoretical investigation has arrived not by patient study on my part (I am a

totalized student of incidentals, pop-ups, and other adventi-
tiousnesses) but by whiffs of intimation already in their fifth
or sixth remove from virtual communication or reception.
But I am still delighted, however amateurishly, because so
much of the philosophical or critical discourse has had at its
center—guess what?—poems, and since I never expected sec-
ondary elaboration or clever stance to do away with what I
feel to be alive at the center of poems (even, sometimes, in
their peripheries, and even when the peripheries spread out
until there seems little if any relation between one iota and
another: not to go on too far with the figure, I mean, for
example, as stars on the outrims of galaxies nearly lose their
orientations with the core), I am peculiarly, perhaps, without
complaint.

I think the thing that got me was when the critics began to
encourage the view of themselves as no longer subject to or
dependent on poems but in a higher register of influx than
poets or poems. I found this particularly amusing because the
critics, having all tried to write poems themselves, had appar-
ently turned to criticism in order to have reason to pursue
literature, a clean and noble calling in which even the grub-
bing is fairly clean and, in many cases, financially rewarding. I
read the poems I could find by the critics, and I pronounced
them not very good. I wondered then just what it is about
critics that enables them to know so much about poetry when
they obviously don't have the faintest idea how it comes about.

But I concluded I was just having a foolish fuss with myself.
There is no reason ever in the world for the critic and poet to
be at odds, and for the following reason: the primary motion
of the poet is to put things together and touch a source that
feels like life—at times even more powerful than life. It is a
synthesis of analogies and associations that promotes, in the
best hands, and even when disjunctive, a sense of renewed
vitality. That is what one feels. That is a fact whether noticed
by poet or critic. The critic makes another kind of synthesis;
his or her synthesis comes as a result of what can be added up
after taking things apart. What is added up, as in dissertations
and works of critical discourse, is thought to be subtler and
finer than the work that gave rise to it. But that cannot be,

because the two modes of thought, the creative and the analytical, are not comparable; they are apples and oranges.

I could go on with this at great length and probably even convince you, if you aren't convinced already, that I am right, but my purpose moves beyond such prideful discriminations.

I am just afraid that young poets have not known how to resist the incursions and mock conquests except by the usual gift of paying no attention to them. I think poets should strive to be ready to counter assaults in any language whatever, and I will try to give you mine, simple and humble as it is.

When exposition has allowed the poem to arrive, its sentences, rhythms, figures coming together or one after the other, the poem ends. At that point, the exposition ceases and the poem stands whole, a disposition of parts, of movement laid out finished and still, like an object. Suppose the object now to be a stone you pick up beside the road and bring to class: you place the stone on the seminar table and ask your students to write about it. Its history can be discussed in terms of the shape its dissolution has taken. A sample can be taken from it for analysis. Its age can be determined. Chronology may be determinable in its layering. In other words, numberless papers, including chemical and atomic notations, can be written, but the stone, apart from its missing specimen, is unaffected. The writings about the stone do not replace the stone. Nothing can replace the stone. It is itself in its own integrity or shambles.

Poems are like that. They come on in a sound stream that cannot be talked away, and any other way of representing the sound stream will not be the same sound stream. Poems to the extent that they are dispositions, not expositions, are nonverbal, just like a stone or a piece of sculpture. Thousands of papers can be written about Rodin and many of them may know more about Rodin than Rodin did but they will not resemble sculpture. Rodin made the sculptures. No one else did.

Until they end, poems exist in time from the first syllable to the last. They are actions. Emerson said that words are a kind of action. Aristotle called drama an imitation of life. Verbal actions imitate human actions or the actions of wind or river or rain. Poems are actions, of which one action is the making of statements. People behave and as a part of that behavior they express opinions, observations, assertions. But the assertion can be the opposite of what the behavior means. If on a January day in upstate New York a person perhaps given to light humor says, "A boiler, isn't it?" you know it's cold outside.

I'm trying not to go on at too great length, but at the same time I risk losing your attention if I don't give you the means to follow me. I say that the behavior of a poem, good or bad behavior, gives us access to a knowledge of the meaning of behavior in our time. For example, a heroic couplet, reasoned and rhymed, is *characteristic* of a certain style of mind and action that identifies a period. A short poem, pure to the exclusion of every challenge, is one style of life. A sprawling, inclusive poem tells us what it is in addition to what it says or says it is.

Value is represented in poems. Poems exemplify ways to behave. We can write poems that disintegrate before the reader's eyes, and by that we can mean that we refuse to respect the values of our day. The poem can be accessible or distraught, harsh or melodic, abstract or graphic, and from these traits we can form our own models and traits.

The question I ask of a poem is: What way of life does this poem seem to be representing? Is it light, witty, lugubrious, generous, mean-spirited? How does it behave? Should I behave that way? If poems are still capable of so strong a communication, however impressionistically derived, am I to think that poetry has become decentered "texts" first of all? Am I to suppose that a sloppy artist is not perhaps advocating sloppiness as a way of life, and isn't it possible that the meticulous poem can be the more beautifully finished the more disgusting? Hasn't behavior perceived early on as bad become the very image of a later good?

Poetry's actions are like other actions. They are at once actions themselves and symbolic actions, representative models of behavior. As long as I have the feeling that poems are capable of evidencing matters of such crucial importance, I will not think that much has changed: poems come from where they always came from; they dance in themselves as they always have; they sing to us as they always will, and we will not need to be told what we feel or which way our inclinations lean or what there is new and lean to find in them. We will dance and sing. Sometime later we will *talk about* singing and dancing, and in that effort, we will need all the help we can get from the critics or anyone else.

"I Couldn't Wait to Say the Word"

I was born and raised on a small farm four miles out in the country from Whiteville, N.C. I was born at home, the nearest hospitals being fairly long journeys away in those days. Three sisters, two surviving, had been born before me, and two brothers, one dying at eighteen months and the other at birth, were born after me. The sister who died before I was born had lived for two weeks.

I was nearly four years old when the Crash came. I have memories of some bright times before the Crash, and later I found old manila envelopes containing records of money we had once had in the bank. But a strict change occurred that was deepened and made permanent by the death of my brother in May 1930. I have images of him lying in his cradle covered with a veil, and I saw his coffin being made, and I watched as he was taken away, his coffin astraddle the open rumble seat of a Model A. I see my mother leaning against the porch between the huge blue hydrangeas as she wept and prayed.

The surviving son, I must have felt guilty for living and also endangered, as the only one left to be next. Mourning the loss of life, in life and in death, has been the undercurrent of much of my verse and accounts for a tone of constraint that my attempts at wit, prolixity, and transcendence merely underscore.

The Depression in the South was bleak. There was no money. There were no coins. We traded chickens and eggs in town for salt, sugar, baking powder, fatback. Cars were beached on wooden blocks, and the tires were transferred to

From *New York Times Book Review,* 17 January 1982.

mule- or horse-drawn carts called Hoover carts. The unpaved roads in my community bore the patterns of unsteady tire tracks. I can almost hear now the sizzle of the tires in sand.

In 1932 I took first grade with Miss Minnie Heaney at the New Hope Elementary School, a wooden structure that stood beside the old New Hope Baptist Church. There were seven grades, seven rooms, each with its wood stove. My sisters and I walked two miles each way to school, my oldest sister's last year in elementary school my first. One game first graders played was fishing for words. The children sat in a tight circle, word cards turned blank side up on the floor, and each student reached in and "caught" a word, which he had to pronounce when he turned the card over. I remember being slapped on the hand and scolded because I couldn't wait to say the word if anyone faltered.

In the second grade, I was the center one day of a good deal of energy and attention on the way home from school. A jealous cousin of mine questioned whether I had actually written the letters of the alphabet on my paper or whether an older person had done them for me. This imputation angered one of my sisters and caused a fury of mutual accusation. I have been impressed with controversy ever since and have avoided it whenever possible.

The only book we had at home was the Bible, and it was almost never touched because it held important documents of births, marriages, deaths—and mortgages and promissory notes. I heard plenty of words at Sunday school and preaching, and I heard the hymns whose words merely went with tunes, but now, as I look back, I see that I heard the meaning of the words, too, because they are the content of my own poems. "Oh, they tell me of a home far beyond the skies"—etc.

In the fifth grade one day, Miss Viola Smith offered an apple to the first pupil who could memorize "In Flander's Field." Ten minutes later, I stood before the class and recited the poem perfectly, and I still can recite it. That year the students drew names for Christmas gifts. I got Daisy Seller's name and knew I couldn't get her a present. But by Christmas, I had a nickel and bought her a candy bar, a "Powerhouse" I think. She cried. Humiliation can find a lot of definition in a single instance.

I was the valedictorian of the small class in seventh grade and delivered a speech in the auditorium. I had scored at the tenth-grade level on the test given at the end of that year. What had happened was Miss Mabel White, later Mrs. Powell, a marvelous teacher. Eighth grade began high school, and we were bused to Whiteville for that. I wrote an essay on miniature cows farmers were trying to breed, and Miss Ruth Baldwin, another splendid teacher, told everyone about it, even seniors. I was elected editor of the school paper, but it— perhaps consequently—never came out.

In tenth grade, I wrote a poem on Pocahontas, and in the navy at the age of eighteen, whisked away to the South Pacific, I began to write poems in a log I kept. After the war in 1946, I enrolled on the GI Bill at Wake Forest College, where the following year I met Phyllis Plumbo, whom I later married. Phyllis moved away for a couple of years but our correspondence included poems to each other, an exchange that deepened the life in words for me. I could I think show a retrospective track of incidents that might have produced me as an artist, preacher, singer, doctor, mycologist, etc., but the string of events I've listed brought me in 1955 to publish through a vanity press my first book of poems, *Ommateum,* and led nine years later to the appearance of my first accepted book, *Expressions of Sea Level,* which was published by Ohio State University Press. Nineteen years elapsed between the time I began to write continually in the South Pacific and the appearance of the Ohio book. They were years of working alone, while working at something else for a living, years in which I received little acceptance or encouragement. But I take no credit for the persistence. Writing poetry is what I did. I had no place else to turn.

II.

Interviews

"The Unassimilable Fact Leads Us On . . ."

Jim Stahl

I'd like to know where you write, how often, when. I read somewhere that you mentioned that you prefer to write "with a lot of noise, things going on around me."[1] Can you talk a bit about where, when, and how often?

It changes. I've lived in the same house here since 1966. I came here in 1964 and then two years later we bought this house. It's a two-story house and upstairs I have a room that is considered *my* room, and there's a typewriter there. It looks out on the backyard—there's a window that looks out over the backyard. That's why I have so much backyard in my poetry. The room on the other side of the house, which I would have preferred, has more sun and looks out over the street. And if I had chosen that room I probably would be a more urbane and contemporary, sophisticated, city-fied poet because I would have been looking toward the city. But from the back room there's a thicket back there so all you see are wild things taking place, if anything takes place at all. I do almost all my writing at home and in that room. At the time I made the statement about loving to write in the midst of things I was indeed writing earlier in my life, and that's where I wrote—in the living room. (A dog, barking loudly outside the office,

This interview was conducted in Ithaca, N.Y., March 13, 1984. It first appeared in *Pembroke Magazine* 18 (1986): 77–85.

interrupts the interview.) We have a liberal dog policy here at Cornell. So I guess partly I was consistent in those days—I wrote on the coffee table in the living room and consequently I was in the midst of the telephone calls and whatever else happened. I didn't find that really troublesome. During the twenty years, almost twenty years, I've been in this house I've raised my son, who is now eighteen years old, and so I've always kept the door open. And he's eighteen now, but during that period he came in and out, and he had his little crises and questions to ask and came in to help me type at times, and things like that. I never felt good about closing the door.

Drafts and revisions of your poems?

I jot down little things—phrases or words or things someone has said—at any time, anywhere, but I never really seriously feel any poem coming together much except at home. What was that about notes and revisions?

I saw a photocopy of one of your poems that had been slightly revised, changes written in. Do you revise a lot or do you try to keep a poem as it comes out the first time?

I believe that my first drafts would indicate that my best poems are almost unrevised. They come almost as they are. And by that I mean, when I say "best" poems, I mean six or eight or maybe ten poems out of the whole. Or maybe a dozen if you stretch the boundaries pretty far. I don't think poets like to claim they've written a dozen great poems. It worries them. But anyway, they mostly come unrevised. But then I go all the way from that point to fifty revisions. I think especially in my early days with my so-called Ezra poems, the very first poems I wrote, I think I may have revised those fifty times. Because I had only a few poems to work with at that time, and if I changed a single word I would want to retype the whole poem so as to see how it looks now. You know, such "extensive" revision has taken place one assumes a different look. The way I work is to keep a folder. And I try to write the whole poem at the first sitting, try to get through something, whatever the precipitation is that's trying to take place. I try to let that happen spontaneously. But then generally I don't try to work on the poem anymore at that time. I just accumulate them in the folder. And then when I have some free time, on the weekend or in the evenings or in the mornings before school, I can take that out and just flip through the poems. And often none of them will interest you, but on occasion a particular one will for some reason stand out, and for me it's sometimes possible, at that moment, to rewrite the poem or to add something to it, to take something out. I feel that I'm back where the poem was. So I'm always working on, I think maybe, literally hundreds rather than dozens of poems at the same time. I've just now this week been revising some poems that I wrote in 1974, and I haven't looked at them since that time. My last book, by the way, has two poems that were written thirty years ago. So, yes, I really think I've covered the gamut about revision all the way from hardly any . . . You know, I have in some of my work tested the possibility of writing spontaneously—getting it "right" the first time—in the long essay poems and in *The Snow Poems*, and earlier in the *Tape for the Turn of the Year* way back in 1963 I tested my ability to say it right the first time in a long poem. And you know that that is an exaggerated test to place on oneself, but if it does come right somehow it has a . . . necessary quality to it that seems inevitable; it seems that there was something taking place in the mind and there was no difference between that and what happened on the page and so it just became itself. Under that sort of tension and rigor, which seems to be very beautiful, often you misfire and it has to be taken out, or revised or something. So I've tried most things. I think poets love to try more than one way. . . . I've tried every way I can think of, if it was interesting to me. Sorry to give you such a long answer to such a short question.

You mentioned your "best" poems. What do you consider your best poems?

I don't really need to do that, do I? I would rather you did that. Don't you think it's fair for someone else to decide what they are? If they are? Supposing there aren't any, and it winds up twenty years from now and I will be saying on the tape, "Harumph, here are my dozen best poems," and no one cares whether I had *one* or not?

How about your favorite poems. Is that a fairer question?

You know, if you will admit this, a writer's favorite poems may not be what he himself regards as his best. Then I would say my favorite poems are maybe the middle range, the more limited and, I don't know . . . A poem that has the possibility of the sizeableness that you would call great suggests a hugeness of appetite or ambition or need or madness or something in the writer that he might be unwilling to accept as his own. As indeed one of my theories is, that poets are as much in flight from the necessity within as they are seeking it out. And, in fact, it may be true that only minor poets are running around trying to find some poetry to say. I don't mean to sound harsh. . . . It seems to me that if you have endured the uncertainty, the anxiety, and so on that Keats identifies as a negative capability, then you would not very likely love that very much; you might want to get away from it and much prefer to go to the beach and have a popsicle. So I don't know what my "great" poems are, if I have any, but the ones I feel comfortable with are the smaller, more concrete, sort of delightful poems. They're sort of like friends. It's more comfortable to be with friends than with some huge person who just came and may suddenly wipe you off the face of the earth with a declaration of some kind or another. No one wants to live with that kind of person.

Would you respond to some quotes from articles about you and statements made by you? "He is neither polemical, esoteric, alienated nor even suicidal. Yet A. R. ('Archie') Ammons has belatedly emerged as a poet of major stature."[2] You spoke a bit earlier about motivation for writing. People like Lowell, Plath, and Berryman were tortured individuals. What makes you write, what is your motivation? Do you feel compelled to write?

I think there are two types of poets, and this won't answer your question completely but nothing could. There is the kind of poet like Lowell and Berryman. Berryman asserts that he would like to get into as troubled a state as possible short of, I guess, suicide because he felt that that would give him the material out of which to write great poems. He was very much in favor of writing "great" poems. And I think it's probably true, from what I've heard of Lowell, that he too jacked the poem up: that is to say he kept hacking at himself and at the poem à la Yeats, for example, in such a way as to get the greatest conflict and density and brutality and energy and tension and whatever else concentrated and focused in the poem. Well, there are two ways, I think. There is, apart from this poet who is constantly trying to intensify, there is the poet who is himself in such an anxious state that he turns to the poem not to create an even more intense verbal environment, but to do just the contrary; to ease that pressure. And this poet is I think potentially the greatest poet. *But,* he must in the very dissolution or effort to ease that pressure, he must not lose it; the reader must know that it's there, that that pressure is there. But the very great poet has such good manners, it seems to me, that he only indicates and touches on, as if to spare the reader more exposure than he can handle. Do you know what I mean? It's a problem of gestures. To me, the really great poet feels as deeply as anyone these matters, but touches only and controls them lightly with delicate gestures that just merely register they are there. To me, the second- or third-rate poet is standing there really sort of uncertain as to whether he feels anything or not and so he begins to bushwhack and hack and cut and try to create an artificial fury because he thinks that will give him the gestures of great poetry, but it gives him just the opposite. Instead of a man standing there with a quietness that he's trying to instill in other people, you see a man loaded with swords and axes and guns—not a proper person. No wonder he can commit suicide. What else is he going to do with all those weapons he's generated? To me, a man who must work himself up, who doesn't believe there's already enough energy in the world to write out of without having to hack his way into some kind of artificial violence, is not a poet.

Is that what you try for—to show what's there without showing too much?

It's not a question of hiding, but if you feel secure enough in the power of what you seem to be feeling you don't have to insist on it. You can understate it and be quiet about it, rather than constantly overstating it. I would like to be, I don't know what I am, but I experience myself as turning to poetry as a way to ease my anxiety rather than to penetrate a flamboyant atmosphere that's going to convince somebody else that I'm a person with deep feeling. I'm not interested in that. And I'm not interested in poets that do that either.

You were quoted as saying, "I write because I have to. Poets write from some need for self expression."[3] *Is that an accurate quote?*

Oh, I don't know. It sounds reasonable.

I don't mean the quote itself. In general.

These things that people say are not always consistent. Don't you find that true of yourself? You wake up one morning and you're sort of in the northwest part of your mind, where you have one nexus or one cluster of associations, in which a certain thing seems right. But a week later you may have moved over to the southwest or somewhere and you have a slightly different perspective. This is not to say that somewhere there isn't a consistent center of thinking—there is—but statements have to be looked at as a certain kind of information. That is to say, it's a discursive or explanatory mode and, consequently, it can never stop. You just go on explaining forever. But the poem is able to become silent, to stop, and it contains within itself the truth that has not been turned into statement, but into a kind of standing, a kind of completion, a theme-like disposition. It's a disposition, a poem is, rather than an exposition. It has a kind of structural integrity that once that's complete then the poem just stands there. It may be made out of words but it's no longer saying anything. It's just complete. Whereas things we then say about that poem, or things we then say about the poet, we can go on saying forever. And they will be more or less true, but they won't represent as nearly the whole truth as this nonstatement thing that's taking place in the poem or in the person. So, I say a good many things about poetry and about poets, and I never intend to misrepresent anything, but I never feel that I have committed myself to saying anything very significant. Because if I wanted to do that or learn anything about that alternative to my poem or someone else's poems for a more complete sense of who that person is or what their identity is . . . There are so many things that happen in a poem that are nonverbal, not just verbal. For example, let's just take one aspect. Supposing you have three poems by a single writer. Indeed, you may locate within each of those poems an area that is no longer represented by words but seems to be represented by tone, pressure, feeling, color, something like that, and then you can impressionistically talk about the effect of that. But if you have three poems by that person, those poems speak to each other in some way in your mind. You'll say, "This poem is almost like that poem, but the difference seems to be this, that, and the other between them." So there's a kind of nonverbal relationship between the three poems which you can also make verbal statements about, but which you can't really duplicate. Do you see what I mean? The relationship between those three poems is nonverbal. There's nowhere that the poet says there is, but nonetheless the relationship is there, because you recognize immediately that the same voice said those three poems. So something nonverbal has been created at the same time something verbal was made. And I think finally the nonverbal assimilations are the things that really draw us to the poems and to the poets. Of course, you could say that you could never get to those nonverbal ones except through verbal means. I think there's the same sort of relationship to motion and stillness in a poem. For example, supposing you begin a poem with . . . you're attracted to an image or a phrase or a rhythm, and the poem starts to do its dance, picking up images and assertion and rhythms as it goes, but then all that motion and that imagery comes still. Well, isn't it interesting that motion should orient itself around stillness?

As verbalism represents a certain amount of silence. And it's when you become still and silent that you feel the whole poem. So anything that I say or have said about poetry is a partial statement, that bearing all the clarity and limitation of definition of statement . . . right? AM I insisting too much?

What I'm particularly interested in . . .

Ah, sex?

No, again some quotes: "What is particularly interesting is that Ammons commands many 'scientific' disciplines besides the literary."[4] *And a quote of your own: "A poem is a configuration with openness. . . . The real poets today, you know, are scientists. . . ."*[5]

Did I say that?

Yes. That's what the Chronicle *article claims. In a book of criticism mention is again made of the scientific:*

> *One way in which Ammons' endorsement of form manifests itself is in his concern with scientific materials. This concern, which is a distinctive feature of his work, is not a matter of drawing on science for metaphors, as other poets might do. Rather, the scientific references that get into his poetry reflect a real attraction to the objects and the processes that concern biologists and physicists, and show as well Ammons' own scientific cast of mind.*[6]

Poems like "Mechanism" and "The Misfit" deal with science. One thing I'd like to know about is sources of metaphors for contemporary poets. What do you consider fair game as far as metaphors are concerned?

Well, I don't use science because I once looked for a source for metaphors, so that the question comes after the fact. Most of my study was in the sciences. I only got a bachelor of science degree, so I didn't do much studying of *any* kind, but I had taken the premed course and then completed my major in science. And after I was out of school I read some sort of ordinary things . . . such as *Scientific American*, things like that.

I was pretty much aware of what was taking place as of late in science. It was perfectly natural for me to speak that way and to write that way. I really was not trying to be scientific, and it was only after the fact that someone said to me that I was the first, among the first—whatever—to introduce scientific terminology into poetry. But I didn't do that in order to introduce scientific terminology into poetry, but because what I knew and understood, and the things that I thought I could see into with some clarity, were deeply informed by the reading I had done and the experiences I had had which you might call scientific.

And there's nothing "unpoetic" about science?

I don't know. I think things right in the center of the humanities can be very unpoetically treated, and I think you can go, on the other hand, to what is considered to be the antipoetic and find there the chief manifestation of poetry. I don't think that there is any kind of prescription or circumscription that should say to a person, "Look here and not there for poetry."

We seem to be eager to place some kind of template or form on every-thing to help us understand. . . .

Well, the whole century as far as I can tell has been a century of explanation. We seem to have taken the view that the truth is to be discovered by the use of the discursive, rational intel-lect. And indeed we do discover some small things along the way, but you would think that after 2500 years we would begin to wonder whether or not the framework provided by the discursive in defining intellect is sufficient to encounter what we think of as reality. And, by the way, there is a piece in the book review this past Sunday where finally some of the liter-ary critics are starting to contest that perhaps poetic truth may be as close to a convincing stance as discursive or analytic definitions of thought. I think they're opposed myself. Some people think they're not. We certainly have had enough of trying to explain away reality, because we've gotten nowhere, as far as I can tell, in 2500 years.

Could you explain "poetic truth"?

Well, of course it doesn't mean that I think there is *a* truth somewhere and that poets are the only ones who have access to it. But I think I mean . . . imitations . . . poetic truth as being a verbalization that is sufficiently comprehensive and rich in its diversity, and sufficiently focused and unified in its point, and accurately enough treated in its gestures and informed enough with its intellect so that as a product it stands believably for us as an imitation of reality. And so we say to ourselves, "Here is the poem that most adequately reflects the feelings I have had in my relationship with the world of reality up until now." That's the poetic truth. For that moment. Later on it might shift some and, of course, we expect it to. But every time we come on such a realization we feel we are . . . well, as Emerson said, we feel sort of that we are more ourselves than we ever have been before. That's the poetic truth. Whereas I think the analytical mind, you know, takes this thing apart and says, "Well, wait. Let's separate it into nine varieties and we'll redefine that." And pretty soon you're down into such small work of analytical nicety that accurate as it might be it has bypassed the subject, which was the more total and comprehensive experience. This seems to be a problem with mind itself. How can you in a single moment of consciousness stay aware of the whole thing you're trying to inquire into *and* inquire into it point by point by point? And so what we often do is we choose one side or another of the situation or we will say, "Forget about generality, let's go after the concrete," forgetting that the concrete is just as much a myth as the transcendental. [The phone rings, interrupting the interview.] That was my partner I play pool with once or twice a week, and we missed it the last couple of days. What else? Is there another question?

Would you read one of these poems from The Selected Poems 1951–1977 *out loud?*

If it's one I can bear I might.

"Jungle Knot"?

Is that the one you would like me to read?

Well, "Mechanism," "Jungle Knot," "The Misfit" . . .

Oh, how about "The Misfit"? I'll read that one, I like that one.
That one goes pretty far towards abstraction. The Misfit [he
begins coughing]. I have a frog in my throat. Have you had
the flu yet this year? I think I have it and it's still in my throat.
[He reads the poem.] This has to do with conventions and
fictions, and single exceptions to that. There have been whole
systems in science that have suddenly become unstable and
questionable because of the single observed new fact. But this
is really a very abstract way of talking about individuals and
societies, I think. In this case the individual would be the
unassimilable fact, the one who will not give over to conven-
tion or the usual style of doing things. And curiously then
he . . . there's the possibility that he could continue to lead the
convention on, because he hasn't joined it completely. So that
each would have to accommodate itself to the other. And in
that shift would be whatever sense of progress we might have.
In the compromise between the individual and the group
there you would get the shift that we would recognize as prog-
ress from whatever change that took place.

*There's a solitary voice in many of your poems. The "Ezra" poems
come to mind.*

Don't you see in these poems a person who has not . . . who
has found it more comfortable to be lonely, to be alone, than
to join into established groups? Because you notice I never
address a group of people. I never seem to think there is such
a thing as an audience, and certainly never try to *reach* an
audience. What I try to do is through the work possible in
writing the poem, I try to create a poem that will come as close
as possible to saying the kind of place I am, where I am and
who I am and what seems to me to be central, and so on. . . .
As a single person. And then my highest hope is that some
equally single, some other person will find that poem and say,
"Yes, this is true for me as well." I'm not trying to lead a mob

for a cause so-and-so in Washington, or to get people to believe in my politics instead of theirs. I would just like to say, as truthfully as I can, what seems to me to be true for me, as an individual, and then *if* that's true for anyone else in the world who happens across my poems then he will recognize it. And then we will know that I am here and perhaps one day I'll find out he's there. And we'll have that. So I do want an audience, but I want them to recognize themselves, wherever they are. One in Montana, one in West Virginia, and one in southern Florida, or wherever they are. And we could all say, "Yes, that feels right for me." Does that answer your question? It *is* a single person.

"Jungle Knot"—could you explain this poem a bit?

Obviously the jungle knot comes at the end, when the snake and the owl are . . . You know, Beebe was a naturalist who did indeed explore the Amazon, and many other things as well. I guess all I'm trying to say is that as with the vine when it grows up the tree, there's a kind of dependence on the part of the vine on the tree. But then if the vine is too successful it kills the tree, and so you have, naturalistically, you have forces in nature and in ourselves and in the mind and in these metaphorical representations of that . . . binds, where one kind of energy is interlocked with another kind and either one destroys the other, or one becomes dominant over the other, or if they are equally matched they destroy each other. But then there's always a mechanism in nature that lets the knot decay. Or a vulture comes down and what was unlockable he unlocks. He takes their eyes out. And that wrestling match is over. That show is over. So that these knots of intertwined energy occur, psychically, physically, outside and elsewhere, and these are some representations of that.

How does this relate to people? That statement in parentheses that you sometimes tackle more than the light shows seems to be more of a general statement. It takes things out of the specific jungle knot and scopes out. How does that apply to people?

I think you've said it. The anaconda came out into the moonlight, isn't it moonlight, isn't it moonlight? on a riverbank so you could see only half of him. The owl, then, misapprehended and thought it was a smaller snake. And so sometimes if you, like an owl, attack a situation you may attack more than just what the light shows. The owl then tried to fly away with the anaconda only to discover it was a lot bigger than he thought. So I guess that's kind of saying to you, look—you better be careful because there may be more to it than just what the light shows.

What inspired this poem?

I don't know. Many of my poems come to me just by beginning, with the first line. It's as if the poem had already dreamed itself whole, but the only way it had to get in to my attention was to stick a little line into my attention, and then once you seize on to the line then you go with it and dream the whole poem out, and there's the poem. It was already there all the time. You just had to give yourself up to it, following it through its unfolding to have it. But that's the way a lot of my poems, it seems to me. . . . I don't think I ever would have written "The Misfit" if it hadn't been "the unassimilable fact leads us on." There's something to it that's attractive to me about that sound, that assertion. Or "it is not far to my place" or "I said I will find what is lowly, and put the roots of my identity down. . . ."

Some of your poems do not use punctuation at all, and some use colons and semicolons. Is that conscious?

Oh, it's absolutely conscious of course, I think. I have read many explanations for it.

Other people's impressions of why you do it? What is the truth?

The truth is just about that complex. I think poems look good without any punctuation. I used to find in the early days, by the way I still do it, that when I begin my poems I begin them with small letters. There's something . . . I really can't . . . It seems too formal to me to begin with a capital letter, or something. It would shut me off completely. I have to sort of feel that what I'm doing is . . . ordinary. It enables me to go ahead with the poem. And also leaving out the punctuation is just an arbitrary piece of perversity that I happen to have a chance there to indulge, and I do it. It's not answering up to . . . sort of what is expected of you in terms of conventions of punctuation. Gives me a chance to be weird, a little weird.

In "Mechanism" a colon allows you to go inside the bird—all the processes, and then come back out of it.

Well, I think I would rather look at punctuation as another variant, where the usages have not been settled and I can move into that and reactivate it in my own terms, make it do what *I* want it to rather than what the rules say. I have said somewhere that I don't like capital letters and small letters because it seems undemocratic for some of the words to get big letters. And also I hate periods because the gap then suggests that one whole sentence has been separated off from the tissue of the whole poem. And I like to think of the whole poem as having a kind of consistency that capital letters would interrupt, and periods would interrupt. But colons, somehow, seem to carry it off, promote it from piece to piece to piece, and I like that kind of evenness and consistency, texture. But I think that these little things, that no one needs to pay any serious thematic attention to, but by such little things you learn a lot about the character of the poems and the person. This odd and weird way he wants to do this thing and the other is his odd and weird way of doing it. You don't like it, you don't have to bother.

Who influenced you? Whom do you like to read?

A person in my position would have read just about everybody. And I think I've been influenced by everybody. Whether or not more by some than others, I don't know. It seems to me I thought it was absolutely astonishing when I first bumped into

Walt Whitman. That must have been a major revelation. Before that I was trying to write Robert Browning monologues because I thought he was terrific. But everybody. I don't read poetry very much now. I have my students. I read their work and I find myself greatly challenged by Mr. Ashbery. Not too many others.

Notes

1. Nancy Kober, "Ammons: Poetry Is a Matter of Survival," *Cornell Daily Sun*, 27 April 1973, 12.

2. A. T. Baker, "Whole Look of Heaven," *Time*, 3 December 1974.

3. "Ammons Expresses Outlook on Poetry," *Cornell Chronicle*, 13 April 1972.

4. From a clippings file at Cornell's News Agency.

5. "Ammons Expresses Outlook on Poetry," *Cornell Chronicle*, 13 April 1972.

6. Alan Holder, *A. R. Ammons* (Boston: G. K. Hall & Co., 1978), 17.

An Interview

William Walsh

I read an interview the other day where the guest was asked if there was a question he had always wanted to answer, but had never been asked.

Most of the questions I have been asked have had to do with literary reputations rather than what I considered the nature of poetry, that is, what is poetry and how does it work? In what way is it an action or a symbolic action? In what way does poetry recommend certain kinds of behavior? Questions like that are of absorbing interest to me. What Robert Bly or somebody else is doing is of no interest to me whatsoever. I've written my poetry more or less in isolation without any day-to-day contact with other writers. Though I have read tidbits in anthologies of other people, I've made no study of anybody else's work, except in school where I read Shelley, Keats, Chaucer, and so on. I like questions that address, if they can, the central dynamics of this medium we work with, not that any answer is possible, but that we meditate the many ways in which it represents not only our verbal behavior but other representative forms of behavior—how poetry resembles other actions such as ice-skating or football. That is to say, I think poetry is extremely important because it's central to other actions, and it should

From *Michigan Quarterly Review* 28, no. 1 (Winter 1989). Reprinted in *Speak, So I Shall Know Thee: Interviews with Southern Writers* © 1990 William Walsh, by permission of McFarland & Co., Inc., Publishers, Jefferson, N.C. 28640.

not be pushed far to the side as a strictly academic study or a technical investigation.

Do you think poetry is threatened by becoming an academic subject?

To the extent that it is a mere object of study, yes. I worry about that, because it means that the action of the poem and the mind, the action of the body of the poem itself, is going to be paraphrased into discursiveness—something is going to be said about it which will be different from the original action. And while I don't know how classes can be conducted any other way, that's not why poems are written. They are not written in order to be studied or discussed, but to be encountered, and to become standing points that we can come to and try to feel out, impressionistically, what this poem is recommending. Is it recommending in a loud voice, extreme action, or is its action small, does it think we should look closely at things, should we forget the little things and look at some big inner problem, should we understate our stances toward the world, or does hyperbole work better, is this a shallow poem, or is there some profound way that it achieves something it didn't even mean to achieve? In other words, we're trying to live our lives and we go to these representative, symbolic actions to test out what values seem to have precedence over others. If human beings in this country or wherever could approach poetry more in that way rather than as a historical or strictly theoretical form of study, then they might feel the ball of strength in poetry and come to it because it would inform and excite them the way Madonna does or punk rock does. Of course, I'm not insisting that poetry become a popular medium. It requires the attention that few people are willing to give it. I kind of wish that weren't so.

Many of the people I've come in contact with who don't read poetry say it's because they don't understand it.

Understanding something has been defined for them as a certain system of statements made about something. If they don't get a very good statement about the poems, it means they haven't opened themselves to the rhythm, pacing, sounds of words, colors, and images that they are supposed to move into. Who understands his own body? I mean the gorillas have been walking around for two hundred and fifty thousand years with extremely complicated enzymic and other operations going on in their bloodstreams that they know nothing about, which prevented them not at all from being gorillas. We're the same case. What are we supposed to understand about poetry? I've studied and worked with poetry since I was eighteen. Poetry astonishes me day after day. I see something else that is somehow implicated in that. I never expect to understand it. You see, there's where the problem is. The kind of understanding that was defined for these people, most people, has been trivial and largely misses the poem.

You spent the first seventeen years of your life in the South, in Whiteville, North Carolina. Could you discuss your background leading up to your first interest in writing?

It covers the period people like to cover in ten years of psychotherapy and don't give up and walk away until they have an answer. [Laughing] I was born in 1926, just toward the end of the good times—the twenties into the Depression. Our family had a pretty rough time on the farm. We had a small subsistence farm of fifty acres on which my grandfather had raised thirteen children, and which in my father's hands became a cash crop farm that was not large enough to raise enough cash. Yet, we didn't do the dozens of things that would have continued it as a subsistence farm. Apparently, my grandfather had done very well. So we were caught in that kind of bind, aggravated by the Depression, about which you've heard endless rumors—all true. [Laughing] It was a rather desperate time until the beginning of the war provided jobs for people, and changes—radical changes. Do you realize that when I was born in 1926 something like 85 percent of the people in the country were rural, lived on a farm, and now it's about 3 percent? So the most incredible silent revolution has taken place just in my lifetime.

After I graduated from high school in 1943 I worked for a

shipbuilding company in Wilmington, then entered the navy when I was eighteen. I was in the South Pacific for nineteen months, came back and entered Wake Forest College in the summer of 1946 on the GI Bill. Nobody in my family had gone to college before. It was a truly daunting experience for me. My major was premed and I minored in English, and then everything collapsed into a kind of general science degree.

You started in a premed program with hopes of becoming a doctor?

Yes, I did. I think it came out of a general interest in things and people and feelings. To be a doctor would have been to get completely out of the mess I was in as a farmer. It was a different social and economic level. I didn't pursue it beyond my undergraduate degree. I had wanted to stay a farmer, but my father sold the farm. So, that option was eliminated. I love the land and the terrible dependency on the weather and the rain and the wind. It betrays many a farmer, but makes the interests of the farmer's life tie in very immediately with everything that's going wrong meteorologically. I miss that. That's where I got my closeness and attention to the soil, weeds, plants, insects, and trees.

Prior to studying English in college had you written very much?

The first poem I wrote was in the tenth grade, where you have to write a poem in class. It was on Pocahontas. Then I didn't write anymore until I was in the South Pacific and discovered a poetry anthology when I was on the ship. Then I began to write experimentally and imitatively. There was a man on ship who had a master's degree in languages and I began to study Spanish with him. We didn't have a text; he just made it up as he went along. It somehow gave me a smattering of grammar—you know how helpful it is with your own grammar to study another language. Pretty soon I was writing regularly. Then I came to Wake Forest where there were no creative writing classes, but I continued to write for four years. About a month before I left Wake Forest I finally got up the nerve to show some of my poems to the professors and they were very encouraging. From then on, my mind, my energies, were focused on poetry even though I had to do what everyone else does—try to figure out some way to make a living.

You didn't begin by sending your poems to small magazines, did you?

I didn't even know they existed. I was just totally ignorant of the literary scene. What a load that is on the mind not to know what the configuration, the landscape of the literary world is. I got married the year I was the principal of the elementary school in Cape Hatteras. From there we went to Berkeley, where I did further study in English, working toward a master's degree. I took my poems to Josephine Miles, a fine poet and critic who died a couple of years ago. She consented to read my poems and said I should send them out. That's where I first heard about literary magazines.

Your first book of poetry, Ommateum, *failed terribly.*

I believe the publisher knew it wouldn't sell and so they only bound one hundred copies of the three hundred sheets pressed. It sold sixteen copies the first five years. Five libraries bought it—Princeton, Harvard, Yale, Berkeley, and Chapel Hill, only because they bought everything. My father-in-law sent forty copies to people he knew in South America. I bought back thirty copies for thirty cents each. So I guess you could say it failed miserably. One review in *Poetry* magazine, my first review, was favorable. But now *Ommateum* goes for about thirteen hundred dollars a copy.

The reason I brought this up is because you did not publish another collection of poetry for nine years. What transpired in those nine years, between the time you wrote Ommateum *and* Expressions of Sea Level, *that produced a resounding critical change in your work?*

We cannot imagine, sitting here, how long nine years is. I just kept writing, resubmitting manuscripts, tearing them apart, putting them back together, getting rejected, trying again, and so on until I was finally rejected by everybody. I took my work to a vanity publisher in New York City and I was turned down by them, too. I went to Bread Loaf in 1961 and met Milton Kessler, who at that time was teaching at Ohio State University. He said their press was starting a poetry series and I should send my poems early on before the hundreds of manuscripts began to arrive. I did and they took it. It was favorably reviewed, but it took ten years for them to sell eight hundred copies. I used to get monthly statements from them saying this month we've sold three copies, this month we sold four. For ten years this happened, and I'm not sure they ever sold all one thousand copies. It is amazing how favorably it was reviewed. I just saw *The Oxford Companion to American Literature,* which has an article on me saying from the day *Expressions of Sea Level* was published, A. R. Ammons was a major poet. . . . Nobody told me then that I was a major poet.

Now, as to what happened to the poetry itself, that's a story so long I wouldn't know how to tell you. I'd have to go back over the stages, the failures, the rebeginnings, and so on. It isn't easy to be a poet. I think if the young poets could realize *that* they would be off doing something else. It takes a long time. It took me a long time. I do believe there are poets who begin right at the top of their form, and usually are exhausted in five years. In a way I wasn't bad either early on. *Ommateum* remains a very powerful influence with me.

Who do you see as starting at the top of their form?

I just happen to think of James Tate, who won a national prize when he was twenty-two. I don't mean to say he burned out. There are poets who seem to be at their best right away. I'm a slow person to develop and change. The good side of that is that it leaves me so much more to do.

When you look back at the poems in Ommateum *as a whole what is your reaction? Do you still feel the same way?*

It's a very strong book. It may be my best book. *Expressions of Sea Level,* though more widely welcomed, more obviously ingratiates itself to an easier kind of excellence. The *Ommateum* poems are sometimes very rigid and ritualistic, formal and off-putting, but very strong. The review I got said, these poems don't care whether they are listened to or not. Which is exactly true. I had no idea there was such a thing as an audience; didn't care if there was. I was involved in the poem that was taking place in my head and on the page and that was all I cared about. If I had known there were millions of people out there wanting to buy my book, which of course is not the case, it would have been nice. But an audience meant nothing to me. Someone else said that I was a poet who had not yet renounced his early poems. I never intend to renounce those poems. [Laughing] I have published some inferior poems in each volume—that's inevitable. But as Jarrell said, if you are lucky enough to write a half a dozen good poems in your life, you would be lucky indeed.

Critics have traced your creative genealogy to several influences: Whitman, Thoreau, Emerson, Pound, Stevens, Frost. One critic stated, "Ammons's poetry is founded on the implied Emersonian division of experience into Nature and the Soul." Would you agree with their findings?

First of all, one has been influenced by everything in one's life, poetic and otherwise. There have been predominant influences, such as Robert Browning, whom I imitated at great length as an undergraduate, writing soliloquies and dramatic monologues, trying to get anywhere near the marvelous poems he wrote. I failed miserably. Whitman was a tremendous liberation for me. Emerson was there in the background; though I am said to be strongly Emersonian I sort of learned that myself. I haven't read him that much. When I read Emerson I see a man far wiser and more intelligent, and a better writer than myself, saying exactly what I would say if I could. That's scary in a way. We're still different in so many ways. But then I do believe I hear, at times, in my poems, distant echoes from every poet, not in terms of his own words, but as a presence. Frost is there, also Stevens. I have read very little Stevens, and basically he's not one of my favorite poets, though I think he's a good poet. They do say of me, even though the influences are there, that my voice remains my own, which is a mystery to me, but apparently it's true. I believe I assimilate from any number of others and other areas. I'm that kind of person—one who is looking for the integrated narrative. That's where my voice finds its capability of movement. It is my voice, but it is an integrated one. Does that sound right?

Oh, yes.

I just made it up. [Laughing]

How, then, would you describe your poetry?

It's a variable poetry that tries to test out to the limit the situation of unity and diversity—how variable and diverse a landscape of poetry can be and at the same time hold a growing center. I have written some very skinny poems you might call minimalist and I've written some very long-lined poems, such as "Sphere." In my early poems I was contemplating the philosophical issue of the One and the Many.

Your poetry deals principally with man in nature, the phenomena of the landscape—earth's nature. I've wondered, because of your scientific background, if you have ever thought about taking man off the earth into space? I don't mean to say science fiction poetry, but into the nature of space.

I don't believe I have, though I've thought a great deal about it—billions and billions of galaxies and billions and billions of stars in each one. Who was it said that if you stick out your arm at the end of space what does it stick into? If space is limited, what happens?

In about 90 percent of your poetry the reader is brought into the poem to witness the solitude of the speaker. Is this solitude your poetic vision of loneliness?

Yes.

Is it your loneliness you're writing about?

Yes it is. I really don't write to an audience. I never imagined an audience. I imagine other lonely people, such as myself. I don't know who they are or where they are, and I don't care, but they're the people whom I want to reach. It seems to me that the people who are capable of forming themselves into groups and audiences have something else to go on besides poetry. So let them go ahead. It could be political, sociological, mystical, or whatever. They're welcome to it and I hope they do a good job, but I am not part of that. I'm really an isolationist. And I know there are others like me. There is some element of ultimate loneliness in each person. In some people it's a crisis. Those are the pieces of loneliness I would like to share at this distance.

You published three major collections in a row: Collected Poems 1951–1971, Sphere: The Form of a Motion, *and* The Snow Poems. *How does this affect a writer's sense that since what you're doing is working, you might as well keep doing the same thing?*

I can't get stuck in a pattern, because I don't believe in patterns. I believe in process and progression. I believe in centralizing, integration, that kind of ongoing narrative, more than I believe in the boxes of identification and completion. That's just the way I am structured as a human being. *The Collected Poems* contains two or three other previously unpublished books. I just dumped them in there. I had them, but didn't want to bother sending them out to magazines.

But *Sphere*, finally, was the place where I was able to deal with the problem of the One and the Many to my own satisfaction. It was a time when we were first beginning to see an image of the earth from outer space on the television screen, at a time when it was inevitable to think about that as the central image of our lives—that sphere. With *Sphere*, I had particularized and unified what I knew about things as well as I could. It didn't take long for me to fall apart or for that to fall apart, too. Thinking of the anger and disappointment that comes from such things . . . I wrote *The Snow Poems*, where I had meant to write a book of a thousand pages. I don't know why I didn't go ahead and do it, because I wanted to say here is a thousand pages of trash that nevertheless indicates that every image and every event on the planet and everywhere else is significant and could be great poetry, sometimes is in passages and lines. But I stopped at three hundred pages. I had worn myself and everybody else out. But I went on long enough to give the idea that we really are in a poetically inexhaustible world, inside and out.

Your work has been anthologized in many publications over the years. They usually publish "Corsons Inlet," "This Is," "Bridge," and "Visit." Of all your poems which do you think is your best work and will most likely survive?

I have always liked two poems of mine that are twins, "Conserving the Magnitude of Uselessness" and "If Anything Will Level with You Water Will" from the *Collected Poems*. I think those are fine poems, but other people don't reprint them. I think anthologists tend to imitate each other. If they find a poem anthologized, they put it in their anthology. I have a great many poems, to tell you the truth, that could just as well have been chosen for an anthology as the others.

Donald Justice said at one time that the United States has not produced a major poet in the last thirty years. Do you agree with this?

I agree with that. The possibility is that Ashbery is a major writer, but other than that I don't know any major writers, except possibly myself. The great poets of the first half of the century are not as great as we thought they were, but they are greater than anything since. I think Eliot was a great poet. I like Ransom a lot. I don't believe Lowell and Berryman are going to prove to be as strong as was thought. I hope I'm wrong about that. It seems to me that there are a million poets that write interesting verse, but I can't think of a single one that I would think of getting up in the morning and going to to find my life profoundly changed and enlightened and deepened by. Not a single one. Isn't that amazing? Or do I just not know about them? I don't mean an answer to life, I mean an encounter of intelligence, sensibility, feeling, vision. Where do I go for a verbal encounter that will be sufficient to cause me to feel that I should come back the next day and the next day to drink from that fountain again?

Do you think we will see a major poet evolve out of the last eleven or twelve years of the century or has the well dried up?

I think not. This century has had it. Like others, I believe that we've been replaying the seventeenth century in which a great deal of poetic energy in the first part of the century dried up into Dryden and Pope. Dryden at the end of the seventeenth and Pope at the beginning of the eighteenth. And we have started to take on a formalist cast now. Maybe we're going to need a century or two before we get back on line.

You've taught at Cornell since 1964.

Yes, that's right. Denise Levertov was poetry editor of *The Nation* and she wanted to take off for six months and she asked me to fill in for her. During that period I accepted a poem by David Ray. I didn't know who he was, but I published his poem. Some months later I was asked to read at Cornell, and it turned out that David Ray was a teacher there. I guess he was glad I published his poem and wanted to meet me. I went to read and they asked me why I wasn't teaching and I said because no one had ever asked me. They proceeded to ask me. I became a full professor in seven years. Some years later Yale made me an offer, so Cornell countered their offer and gave me an endowed chair. They have just honored me beyond all dreams. I teach part-time . . . one course that meets once a week. It's like having your life free. I go over every day and talk to students and go to meetings, but I don't have to.

Is it stimulating for your work to meet with the students everyday?

Not much any more. I need human contact, but it needn't be profound. To see someone and have a cup of coffee really restores me. See, I don't like to live alone. I don't think that I'm much of a teacher, but that's not what the students tell me. I never feel very competent. I don't think anyone who teaches poetry can feel very competent, because the subject is so over-whelming and it's easy to miss the center of it. Can you imagine in a creative writing class the interplay between the teacher and the student—how complex that is on both sides? Superficial, no matter how profound. It's so superficial and so mixed, "Help me, don't help me. Criticize this poem but only say good things. Don't tell me what my next move is. Tell me, but don't let me know that you told me what my next move is, so it will seem that I discovered it for myself. When I owe you some-thing please be the first one to say I owe nothing." That is to say, the relationship is extremely complex and draining on that account. You would have to be superhuman to know what to do in that situation. I am, as it turns out, not superhuman. But they say I'm a good teacher, nevertheless. I do the best I can. I must say that I have a pretty quick eye on a poem. I can tell what it is likely to amount to or not amount to rather quickly. It's just a wonderful job, but I'm tired of it, only because of something they call "burnout." After having done something for twenty-five years I don't know what happens. I guess you begin hearing yourself say the same thing, repeating yourself.

When I first began to teach, I would go into the classroom and see eighteen or twenty individuals and I believed they were individuals. After about five years of teaching six courses per year, I would come into a writing class knowing full well that there were three or four basic problems. Diction—there is al-ways too much poetic diction. There's the problem of shape, or the lack of it—some contact with an ideal form. There's the problem of consistency. It's not sufficient to have a good line and a good image, you need to write a whole poem. Then, as a teacher, you have to begin to nudge yourself and say, "This person sitting in front of you is not an example of one of these problems, he's a person." After awhile, if you have to nudge yourself too much, then it's time to quit.

If the burnout begins to weigh too heavily upon you, is there something that you would prefer doing instead of teaching?

I would like to, now, be designated, as anything in this world, POET. Not teacher, not professor, not farmer, but one who writes poems. What I would like to do now, since I have not allowed myself to do it in twenty years is to go out and meet the people who read my poems. I have been giving poetry readings lately which I did not do for a long, long time. I would like to stay home when I go back to Ithaca and write my poems, send them to magazines, go see people, because I don't know how to tell somebody else how to write.

You don't categorize yourself as particularly Southern, a Southern writer.

I feel my verbal and spiritual home is still the South. When I sit down and play hymns on the piano my belly tells me I'm home no matter where I am. So, yes, I am Southern, but I have been away from the immediate concerns of the South a long time. I guess we should define Southerner. Who are Southerners? Are they white, black? Does a black Southerner want to be separated from a Northerner? Does he feel the same boundary in the North as the Southerner often does? Also, the South has changed so much demographically, that it's difficult to know. I was just in the bank the day before yesterday and I told a young lady I was going back home to Ithaca. She had just moved down from Kingston, New York. She said she liked it, but missed the snow. At the next teller's window was a woman who said she was from New York. So there we were, the three of us, adjacent to each other from New York. The very same thing happened in the post office one morning.

How does a poet deal with this change?

I wonder. I don't think it has very much effect on me. The sources of poetry, by the time you are as old as I am, sixty-two, have taken all kinds of perspectives, and while the work may be changed in tone and mood by recent events, it's changed only slightly. Curvature of the narrative, by that time, becomes fairly well established, and while it can change, it won't change much.

You never dreamed of becoming a poet in the sense of receiving recognition for your work. You thought of yourself as being an amateur poet and not a "Poet." Once you began publishing , when did you begin to think of yourself as a "Poet"?

When I said amateur poet, I meant that I didn't want to professionalize it. It seems to have more spontaneity, immediacy, and meaning to me when I think of it as just something I do. I worry when poetry is professionalized. I think maybe I am a poet. I keep getting letters from all over the world from people who say they are moved by this and that. Whatever it was that they were moved by is in the past for me. I just wrote a poem this morning. That's where I'm at. I try to live each day as I can. If I write a poem, fine. If I don't, that's fine. I think life ought to come first. Don't you? One is alive in the world with other people. I write poetry. Other people collect insects or rocks. I don't think I have answered this question very well, but you know how at some point in your life you have meditated deeply on a subject—you remember that you have meditated on it, you file it, and the next time you try to remember it you can't access it. You have to take thirty minutes to work your way there, then you might have something to say, or you might not. That's what just happened. [Laughing]

Do you think there are writers, poets, who take poetry too seriously, that they feel poetry is almost more important than life?

The solemn, the pompous, the terribly earnest are all boring.

We touched upon your childhood earlier and I'd like to ask if you have a favorite childhood memory?

I remember one Christmas when I got a little tin wagon with milk cans drawn by a mule or a horse. I must have been five or six. I remember getting back into bed and playing with that on top of the quilt, thinking it was absolutely marvelous.

Turning this around, do you have a least favorite childhood memory?

The most powerful image of my emotional life is something I had repressed and one of my sisters lately reminded me of. It was when my little brother, who was two and a half years younger than I, died at eighteen months. My mother some days later found his footprint in the yard and tried to build something over it to keep the wind from blowing it away. That's the most powerful image I've ever known.

Throughout your career you've professed formlessness and boundlessness. Have you found either?

I guess the other side of that question is, is there anything, in fact, in our world and perception that isn't formal in one way or the other? I guess not. The air between me and that oak tree is invisible and formless. I can't see the air. So I see nothing but form out the window. I know the air is there because I see it work on the trees, and so I begin to think there is an invisible behind the visible, and a formlessness, an ongoing energy that moves in and out of a discrete formation. It remains constant and comes and goes and operates from a world of residual formlessness. That space, at some point, develops what we perceive. In a way I have experienced the idea of formlessness and boundlessness, but these are imperceptible thanks to our senses.

For the last three or four months I have been profoundly occupied with the conceptual aspect of poetry—poetry that has some thought behind it. But also, the poem is a verbal construct that we encounter, learn from, make value judgments with, and go to to sort out possibilities in relation to our own lives in order to try to learn how to live. I'm sick and tired of reading poets who have beautiful images that don't have a damn thing to say. I want somebody who can think and tell me something. You reintegrate that into a larger thing where you realize that thought and loss are certainly not the beginning and end to things, but are just one element in the larger effort we are making, which is to try to learn how to live our lives.

Perversity, Propaganda, and Poetry
Zofia Burr

Not originally designed as an interview, this discussion took place over the course of two days in 1993. On May 31 we spoke in Ammons's office in Goldwin Smith Hall at Cornell University, and the next day we spoke in his home. Many of the questions and issues that arise here had been at stake in our conversations since the fall of 1984, when I entered the M.F.A. program at Cornell.

May 31, 1993
In what sense is your poetry a matter of communication, of addressing a listener?

Well, I think one of the more perceptive statements ever made about my poems was made by Helen Vendler when she said that "never has there been a poetry so sublimely above the possible appetite of its potential readers." I think she means by that that the poems are addressed to nobody. So I was thinking, isn't that an interesting form of address when you don't address anyone. And I would think that this is an important part of what poetry makes possible. There it seems that all conventional means of addressing someone have been put aside and yet the pressure to communicate a presence is never greater or more successfully done.

I have coffee sometimes in the morning for years with people. And then it may be five or ten years afterwards they will show me something they've written and I will suddenly feel that I know them better in that minute than I have known them through all the conversations that had taken place before. And this is not to dispute the value of conversation, but to say that there's something about the poem, the rest of the poem, that communicates a person's gait—I wonder if I'm deluded about this—and that allows you to get somehow deeper into the nature of that person, the essential nature of that person, than you can through conversation, which tends to be more discursive.

As you say in "A Note on Prosody," as a poet you are—at least initially—both the speaker of the poem and the listener. And that accounts for your experience, as a reader, of getting something more full from listening to someone speaking within the poem than from conversation. Of course, I would argue that that's a fiction. It's a useful fiction. It's a really useful fiction for poetry because there're so many situations in which you have things to say to people but you can't actually say those *things to* those *people. Right?*

Yes. But when you use the word *address,* I think you're admitting about yourself that you're interested in personal relationship. And most people are. But I wrote in such a vacuum for most of my life. Address didn't seem to be important. As Helen Vendler says it, I didn't seem to be wanting to say anything to anybody.

But do you really think that's the case, that you don't want to say anything to anybody? I can understand that the poems may appear as if they don't care whether anybody listens to them. Well, that's one thing. But I don't think that's the same as: "Archie Ammons doesn't want to say anything to anybody."

Well, let me put it another way. With me, when I'm writing a poem it seems like there's a phrase that's sort of in my mind that I begin with. But it just seems to me that I'm there to follow it, and it just turns around and it comes out at the end, often totally surprising to me where it comes out, you know? But it seems like my attention has been focused on something like dynamics or something, or how this poem is going to work, how this poem is going to find its way, how it's going to find its way rather than whether or not it's speaking to anybody in particular.

But it seems to me that actually an enormous amount of speaking goes on in this very indirect way.

I'm wondering about your experience teaching creative writing. Could we talk about that?

I had the M.F.A. workshop at Cornell this spring, and there are some very good writers there. But the drive to be unintelligible, to be very difficult, is so strong that we were almost compelled to begin by trying to find out the disposition of the poem and how the parts did or did not work together and whether or not it meant to be coherent or incoherent, whether it meant to make statements or just jabber, and whether or not it's centered around any cluster of images or a relationship between one image and another. You know, it really was difficult to read these poems.

But that sounds like a worthwhile process.

Well, yes. But when students, having taken some workshops, begin to see that that's the way poems are approached, then they begin to write puzzles that will cause more discussion and more wrenching of the spirit to see what's there. Frequently by the time you clear it up all the energy is gone.

Right.

And there's nothing there. There's no residual feeling. It's been used up. The simplest poem in the world is also a puzzle. Jonathan Culler, trying to refute M. H. Abrams, uses that couplet by Frost: "we go round, go round and round," and "we don't know anything, but the secret sits in the center." Culler just takes those two lines, which are perfectly clear, as for their direct content, but then he begins to find complication after complication, so that ultimately the poem, like every other, turns into a puzzle. Often creative writing students set out to create puzzles.

Would that apply to you?

No, no, no.

Not at all?

No.

And yet that would seem to me to resonate with how you understand what Helen Vendler said about your first book, in that it was "above" the listener?

Well, I suppose I'm just too old-fashioned to talk here, but I always thought that the poet should be deeply enough involved in the complexity and many-sidedness and depth of things, that he would be naturally struggling for some sort of clarification, and that then he would put his whole effort into creating a model that would show how some clarification runs through this multiple structure of things. That a person could know something rather clearly, and deliberately complicate it, is absolutely foreign to me. And yet I think twentieth-century poetry has aimed at distortion rather than clarification. What I'm aiming toward is clarification but at the same time inexhaustibility. The deconstructionists talk about the multiplicity of a work, its soliciting. But that sounds as if they're making negative what I always consider as positive. What's positive about a poem is that it can be clear in the way it structurally or procedurally sets itself up, and yet absolutely inexhaustible in its suggestiveness. You can approach it from so many different sides. Is that not true? And so I always thought that you can be clear about a poem, clear enough to see how it disposes itself, and yet it can invite you to consider more and other aspects of things, so that you learn from it. But the very idea of deliberately taking something that was clear and making it obscure seems to me perverse. And I'm a very perverse person myself, so I'm not blaming perversity. It's just, *that* to me sounds perverse.

It seems to me you're talking as if you care about saying something to people. When we began this conversation, I understood you to say that you yourself really didn't have a reader in mind. But you do have a thing that you want to say, that you want to share. And you want people to get that.

I do, but at the same time to feel that they haven't got it all, that it's inexhaustible, that this is just a sort of a structural clarification of very complicated matters. But I think that my students think of clarity as being simplification. And I also think they're terrified of feeling of any kind, because they think it will be mistaken for sentimentality.

If you heard somebody walking down the hall and you couldn't see them, and you recognized that you knew that person from the way he walked, you would know all kinds of things about the statements that person would make when you did see him, and you would have memories. Well, if you knew the work of a poet, it would be the same way. You hear this clunking thing going on. You say, "Oh, I know who that is." And that's not a mystical thing. Those things are just as real as the words are.

June 1, 1993
I want us to step outside our personal uses of the poem, and into the poem itself somehow.

Well, I want that too—I mean I want the poem to be listened to in and of itself, as much as possible. But I also think that we have to work on acknowledging the kinds of investments we're bringing to our reading. I don't think we can just disregard that we have things at stake in reading.

Yes, well, there is a difference between us here. It's not a big difference. I think mainly we agree. It's just the way everybody has a different disposition toward things. But we were talking yesterday about *not knowing* what use you're going to make of yourself, or what the world's going to be, and you expose yourself to the arising or emerging of the poem on its own terms if possible. And, for example, when I think of

Adrienne Rich, I think of a very fine poet, but of a person who has certain programs to promote, certain areas of interest that she wants to promote. And that feels propagandistic to me. It feels to me as if she imposes those burdens on the poems she's writing before the poem has a chance to make its own emergence. The most precious thing to me about a new poem is that it be unconditional, that it not be prelimited, or predirected, by some interests of my own, but that I try to disabuse myself of all interests, with the hope that there will be some originality of perspective, or content, that will arise without my being able to anticipate it. I mean, that would be what creativity is—creating something you didn't know before. So I want to disable my own interests in the poem, except that, of course, I'm there. I am the one who's writing the thing, but the fiction is that I am trying to have it emerge as itself first, and then I will make whatever use I please out of it—but that I mustn't put any limitation or imposition on it, as a program, as propaganda, as an issue first.

But you realize that that's a position that you're allowed to inhabit because of who you are.

No, I don't realize that. How do you mean that?

For instance, when I write something, when I write a poem, in whatever I write, nobody imagines that it is disinterested, because I have an identity that is marked as interested because I am a woman.

Well, I'm a man.

You're a man, but that's an identity that exists as if it is unmarked in this culture. You're a white, straight, man. You're educated. You teach in an Ivy League university.

I'm not as untroubled as you think.

I know you're not untroubled. I know you well enough to know that you're quite troubled.

Right.

But I know that, or I'm arguing that, the idea of a position that is not invested is really a privilege. It's a very useful privilege. It's a privilege everybody should get to have. But the thing is, if you have moved around in the world and nobody has ever taken anything you did as disinterested, because of who they perceive you to be, then you just can't take that position. I can't take that position. And Adrienne Rich can't take that position, and a whole lot of poets can't take that position.

Well, I have interests, as you have interests. The way that I address them, though, is not poetically. It seems to me that if I wrote a letter to the editor of the *Ithaca Journal,* it would be read by twenty thousand people. I could write it overnight. But if I write a poem, it will be read by three people in Wisconsin, or somewhere. That is not an effective way, in my case, to present my personal interests.

But it's not a matter of straightforwardly presenting a matter of personal interest, but to admit that you have *an interest. To admit that you have an investment, even if that investment is to appear as if your investments aren't in the fore.*

Well supposing, instead of thinking of the poems you write as being an identity you have, or wish to expand, supposing you just thought about poetry and wrote and became a major poet. I mean a great, major voice. I know that such things are an embarrassment in our time, but supposing you did, then you could promote your issues much more effectively. You could get on the air and say "It's true I'm a great poet, but let's forget about that. What I'm really interested in is helpless people, or poor people around the country, or whatever."

You're reducing the idea of an interest very much here.

Yes, I do think of it as a limited thing.

And I don't think of it as a limited thing.

That's a very important point.

I don't think of the fact that people have investments in things as a disability. Now I know that this is the way we're trained to think. If somebody is invested in something that they're talking about, we give them less authority. This is something that we're trained to think. And the idea of a disinterested poem works very nicely in line with that.

Well, I told you I was old-fashioned.

*Well, this is how my students think, too, and it is the way I was taught to think. But in my experience, what that means is that people who don't have the privilege in whatever situation they're in to be per-*ceived *as uninvested can't take that stance. So there's no point to it for me.*

Well, you know the traditional response to this is, "If you're interested in these things, why don't you go into politics, or political science, or psychology?"

Right, but it's politics at the level of how things work and how we think about things, and that seems very appropriate in the poem. I mean there is a politics to what you were saying yesterday about clarity. You say, "I always thought that the poet should be deeply enough involved in the complexity and many-sidedness and depth of things that he would be naturally struggling for some sort of clarification—"

Yes.

"—and that then he would put his whole effort into creating a model that would show how some clarification runs through this multiple structure of things."

That sounds pretty good.

Now, it sounds to me like that's a politics.

What kind of politics does that sound like?

That's a way to approach the world, a way to approach things, a way to think about things. "I think the poet has a responsibility to advocate a certain kind of clarity." That seems to me like an investment, a completely legitimate kind of investment.

But it's not spelled out in the terms of an issue or program.

No. But see, I don't think that investment comes just from your intentions. As I was saying before, a lot goes on in the world and in relation to our poems that has to do with who we're perceived to be, and the fact that I am a woman and a poet means that this poet-ness is always marked by that. It doesn't matter whether I announce it or not. If I am read that way, I am read to be invested that way. And you're read to be invested in the things that your identity is bound up with, Southerness, and so forth, and it doesn't matter whether you put that there, or not.

It's imposed.

It's imposed, but as we were saying yesterday, it's pretty hard to get outside all of that stuff. I mean it's important to try, to try to imagine things differently, and that goes back to people starting to write out of an urge to be understood in a context in which no understanding is possible—like children, for instance, writing poems to adults who would never just listen to them say what they have to say. And I think that's the thing with the poem, we can create a space in which as a speaker we have authority.

Okay, you have perceived in your world that a change is taking place in the way women poets are viewed as poets and as women, and you wish to enter into that stream of energy, and cause some things to happen. You would like to see women poets in a state of equality with male poets. That would be a given. But you would also like to see more women poets more strongly and vigorously entering into the world of poetry. Is that correct? Is that one of the things that you feel that you'd like to see happen? Is it that you think women poets are not taken on an equal basis now, and that hurts? What hurts?

The issue for me is not women in particular, although as a woman poet I am taken up into that "stream of energy" as you call it. What I'm really interested in is having everybody who is writing and talking admit that they're invested in something.

Why is that so important?

Because it seems to me that everybody is interested in something. Everybody is promoting something.

I would have taken that for granted, I think.

But some positions are treated as if they're not positions.

Yes. Well, there are positions, on the one hand, and the way they're described, on the other. And we all have positions, but you could describe the position as propaganda. I think that you would like me to say that I'm invested in something, and I'm sure I am, but to tell you the God's truth, I don't know what it is. And however I'm perceived by other people, I don't agree with them—except for those who think my poetry is worthless, because I think it's worthless, too.

I mean, you're saying that I'm some kind of white male straight whatever creature that has no doubts. I know you don't mean to say that.

No, I don't think that anybody has "no doubts."

I'm as afflicted with all kinds of doubts and all kinds of sharings of mortality with others and the need for love and the lack of it and all these things, just like everybody else. And I never think of myself as being superior to anybody. Quite the contrary. Even with you, I feel that what you're trying to tell me and will tell me, is something that I very much lack and very much need to know, and wish to find out. But I don't know what my investment is. I'll bet you could see it better than I could.

Yes, I think that that's probably almost always true.

Under the little shell that we go by day to day, for everybody, there is such turmoil and confusion. We really need to spend a little more time, I think, not sympathizing, not empathizing either, just tolerating. That's a terrible word. Realizing that people have to come up with defining shapes of themselves day to day in order to deal with the world. But underneath that fiction, useful as it is, is a multipurposed, laboring, frightened, happy, sad cluster of circumstances, and this is true for all of us and we all need all the help we can get.

I completely agree. I mean we all need all the help we can get, but I guess what I'm trying to get at is nothing about you or me in particular, but about the fact that when something's said, it matters who seems to be saying it.

Give me an example.

Say for instance, if there was a line in a poem—let's see—"I always thought that the poet should be deeply enough involved in the complexity." Say that were the opening of a poem. Now, if you perceive—now maybe not you—but I am saying that in my experience of people reading, who they perceive that speaker to be will determine how they take that first assertion. And some people have the authority in given circumstances—I mean authority doesn't stay with you wherever you go and for all time—

I'm sure you have to earn it or it wouldn't be granted to you at all.

Yes, you have to earn it, but there are also identities—

Offices, offices. You step into the office and your voice resonates with the size of that office, like Bill Clinton or George Bush.

Right. The office of a poet is very important for everybody—everybody can use that office somehow because it does have something.

But it's by being out of that office that you can size it up, relate yourself to it, sometimes just as much as by identifying with it.

But if you inhabit certain identities in certain places, it's easier, or harder. Right?

Okay.

That's all I'm saying. There are contexts in which my voice would have more authority than yours—

Absolutely.

—and there are contexts in which your voice would have more authority than mine.

And there's the whole equivocal issue of who is in a happier position, the one who finds it easy to say these things, or the one who finds it hard to say them. The one who has less authority and for whom it's more difficult to speak will very likely engage a denser, more realistic set of terms than will the one who finds it easy to say something.

Well, you don't find it easy to say things?

I don't think so. I always feel uncertain about what I'm saying, so it's never easy. I'm always feeling, whatever I'm saying, that I don't really believe it, and that maybe in the next sentence I'll get it right, but I never do. And I think it's because I'm always trying to speak the unspeakable, but that's the only thing that's interesting. Why speak the speakable? That's easy. That's what I mean. It's easy to speak the speakable. But how do you bring your attention to the unspeakable and then say that? That's difficult. And you don't know what's going to emerge. I guess that's the position I'm from, rather than these given entities of things that you just deal with and move around in different sets. Like Coleridge—you go to a territory where it has not yet been spoken. And you don't know how to speak that either. And then you begin to try to say what it is and where you are.

The *Paris Review* Interview

David Lehman

One day in the winter of 1987 Archie Ammons was driving north on the I-95 in Florida when a gigantic hill of rubble came into view. The sight sparked an epiphany: "I thought maybe that was the sacred image of our time," the poet said. Upon his return to Ithaca, New York, where he is the Goldwin Smith Professor of Poetry at Cornell University, Ammons tried to write a long poem entitled *Garbage*. Nothing came of the first attempt. Two years later, however, the image returned and wouldn't let him off so easily. He wrote the poem quickly, finished it in a season, then put it aside. A major medical predicament—a massive coronary in August 1989 and triple by-pass surgery a year later—intervened. When Ammons returned to the poem, he was no longer sure of it, and when it was accepted by his publisher, he was surprised. Nobody else was when this extraordinary work went on to win the 1993 National Book Award in poetry, the second time Ammons has been so honored. Shortly after Ammons received the Frost Medal from the Poetry Society of America, and in October 1994, he and his wife, Phyllis, drove to Washington (the Ammonses do not believe in flying) to collect the Bobbitt prize, which sounds like something a Court TV reporter made up but is actually an accolade bestowed by the Library of Congress.

From an unpublished piece commissioned by *The Paris Review*, November 1994.

Born in Whiteville, North Carolina, in 1926—"big, jaundiced and ugly," in his words—Archie Randolph Ammons grew up on a family tobacco farm during the meanest years of the Great Depression. He had two sisters; two brothers died as infants, losses mourned in his powerful poem "Easter Morning." The hymns Archie heard every Sunday in church had their mostly unconscious influence on his poetry, which he began writing in the Navy during World War II. Some of his first efforts were comic poems about shipmates aboard the destroyer escort on which he served in the South Pacific. Ammons recently wrote the poem "Ping Jockeys" when he found out that two pillars of the New York School of Poets, James Schuyler and Frank O'Hara, had also been trained as sonar men on Key West, where Ammons learned "how to lay down depth-charge patterns on enemy hulks."

Ammons got out of the Navy in 1946. He was able to attend college thanks to that piece of enlightened social legislation, the G. I. Bill, which paid his way at Wake Forest University, where he began as a premed student. In a writing class taught by E. E. Folk, he learned his method of "the transforming idea"—how to organize materials gathered from disparate sources—which he has continued to use in his poems. Another course with a decisive impact on Ammons's life was intermediate Spanish, which was taught by Phyllis Plumbo, a recent graduate of Douglass College, then the woman's division of Rutgers University. Archie walked her home one day and the couple recently celebrated their 47th wedding anniversary.

Ammons did not enter the academic life until he was close to forty. In 1949, he became the principal of the tiny elementary school in the island village of Cape Hatteras. For most of the next decade he worked as a sales executive in his father-in-law's biological glass company on the southern New Jersey shore. Ammons published *Ommateum,* his first book of poems, with Dorrance, a vanity press, in 1955; a mere sixteen copies were sold in the next five years. (A copy today would fetch two thousand dollars.) He joined the Cornell University faculty in 1964 and has taught there ever since.

Expressions of Sea Level, Ammons's second collection, came out in 1964 from Ohio State University Press and triggered off the most prolific period in his career. He went rapidly from total obscurity to wide acclaim. His prematurely-entitled *Collected Poems 1951–1971* won the National Book Award in 1973. He won the coveted Bollingen Prize for his long poem *Sphere* (1975), in which the governing image was the earth as photographed from outer space. Ammons's method for writing a long poem is, in a nutshell, finding "a single image that can sustain multiplicity."

For a poet who believes in inspiration and spontaneity, Ammons is a creature of fixed habit. He begins his days having coffee in the Temple of Zeus, a coffee bar on the Cornell campus, with a handful of chums such as the Nobel Prize-winning chemist and poet Roald Hoffmann. (Hoffmann, who has written two books of poems, unabashedly calls Ammons his guru.) Archie professes to despise the poetry writing industry and has a skeptical attitude on the whole question of whether poetry can be taught. Yet his own reputation among students past and present is high. A casual exchange of poems with Archie can turn into a memorable experience. "I have coffee sometimes in the morning for years with people," Ammons says. "And then it may be five or ten years afterwards they will show me something they've written and I will suddenly feel that I know them better in that minute than I have known them through all the conversations that had taken place before."

This interview was conducted by a variety of means. We began with two long sessions with a tape recorder in Ammons's house in Ithaca. Briefer exchanges in person, on the phone, and by mail followed at regular intervals. It was as if we were continuing a conversation that had begun in 1976, when we met, and of which this interview is a sample and a distillation. We shelved it for a while while we worked together on *The Best American Poetry 1994*, for which Archie made the selections, and then we picked up where we had left off.

As Ithaca neighbors Archie and I lunch together often. Once we arranged to meet at a locally celebrated Thai restaurant (my choice). When it turned out to be inexplicably closed, Archie suggested that we go instead to Tops, a giant supermarket nearby, where we could choose our lunch from the salad bar and eat it at one of the little tables in the deli section. The prospect excited him. Another time we were celebrating his birthday at Friendly's (his choice). Ammons told me he'd been having trouble sleeping. "I used to be in love with the unconscious," he said wistfully. "I used to lie down and go to sleep and sleep through the night." Aren't you going to ask me some *Paris Review* interview questions, such as "What do you write with or on?"

All right. [Pause] What do you write with or on?

My poems begin on the typewriter. If I'm home—and I rarely write anything elsewhere—I write on an Underwood standard upright, manual, not electric, which I bought used in Berkeley in 1951 or '52. It had been broken and was rewelded. It's worked without almost any attention for forty-three years. When I was away a few times, for a year or summer, I wrote on similar typewriters. It's hard now to find paper and ribbons.

I sometimes scribble words or phrases or poems with a pen and pencil if I'm traveling or at work. But I like the typewriter because it allows me to set up the shapes and control the space. Though I don't care for much formality (in fact, I hate ceremony), I need to lend formal cast, at least, to the motions I so much love.

When you begin a poem, do you have a specific source of inspiration, or do you start with words and push them around the page until they begin to take shape?

John Ashbery says that he would never begin to write a poem under the force of inspiration or with an idea already given. He prefers to wait until he has absolutely nothing to say, and then begins to find words and to sort them out and to associate with them. He likes to have the poem occur on the occasion of its occurrence rather than to be the result of some inspiration or imposition from the outside. Now I think that's a brilliant point of view. That's not the way I work. I've always been highly energized and have written poems in spurts.

From the god-given first-line right through the poem. And I don't write two or three lines and then come back the next day and write two or three more; I write the whole poem at one sitting and then come back to it from time to time over the months or years and rework it.

Did you write, say, "The City Limits" in one sitting?

Absolutely.

The eighteen lines of that poem do seem to be a single outcry. Were there changes after you wrote it?

Hardly a one. I sent the poem to Harold Bloom, something I almost never had done, and he admired it and he sent a note to me not to change a word.

Bloom has been a long-time champion of your work. How long have you known him?

He was here for the year in 1968, and his children were the same age as my son John, and they became playmates. Harold and I became friends. I didn't regularly send him my poems and he never suggested how they be written. But I wrote "The City Limits" and I wanted to share it with him. It was not literary business. It was friendship business. That was in 1972.

Where does inspiration come from? Scratch that; let me put it a different way. Does inspiration originate in nature, in external reality, or in the self?

I think it comes from anxiety. That is to say, either the mind or the body is already rather highly charged and in need of some kind of expression, some way to crystallize and relieve the pressure. And it seems to me that if you're in that condition and an idea, an insight, an association occurs to you, then that energy is released through the expression of that insight or idea, and after the poem is written, you feel a certain resolution and calmness. Well, I won't say a "momentary stay against confusion" (Robert Frost's phrase), but that's what I mean. I think it comes from that. You know, Bloom says somewhere that poetry *is* anxiety.

Bloom talks about the anxiety of influence, but you talk about the influence of anxiety.

Absolutely. The invention of a poem frequently is how to find a way to resolve the complications that you've gotten yourself into. I have a little poem about this that says that the poem begins as life does, takes on complications as novels do, and at some point stops. Something has to be invented before you can work your way out of it, and that's what happens at the very center of a poem.

What poem are you referring to?

It's called "The Swan's Ritual" or something like that. It's in the *Collected Poems*.

I used to have this picture of you taking long walks along some places mentioned by name in your poems such as Cascadilla Falls here in Ithaca or Corsons Inlet on the New Jersey Shore, and writing as you were walking, or writing as you reached a plateau or a bridge, writing out something longhand.

Or memorizing it in your head.

Did you do that?

Yes, oh yes. Not something as long as "Corsons Inlet" but shorter poems. I've done that here in Ithaca and down there many times.

"Corsons Inlet" is 128 lines long. Did you write "Corsons Inlet" at the end of the long walk described in the poem?

Yes, and at one sitting.

A poet of inspiration, a poet who depends on inspiration, isn't likely to write on schedule, and I don't suppose you do.

No, I never sit down or stand up to try to write. It's like trying to go to the bathroom when you feel no urge. Unless I have something already moving through the mind, I don't go to the typewriter at all. The world has so many poems in it, it has never seemed to me very smart to force one more upon the world. If there isn't one there to write, you just leave it alone.

Why do you write?

I write for love, respect, money, fame, honor, redemption. I write to be included in a world I feel rejected by. But I don't want to be included by surrendering myself to expectations. I want to buy my admission to others by engaging their interests and feelings, doing the least possible damage to my feelings and interests but changing theirs a bit. But I think I was not aware early on of those things. I wrote early on because it was there to do and because if anything good happened in the poem I felt good. Poems are experiences as well as whatever else they are, and for me now, nothing, not respect, honor, money, seems as supportive as just having produced a body of work, which I hope is, all considered, good.

It took you a long time to get respect, honor, money, and fame for your work. You had the support of Josephine Miles when you were a graduate student at Berkeley, and you had poems accepted by Poetry *magazine in the 1950s. But you had very few readers, and you weren't winning a lot of prizes and grants.*

That's right. I spent twenty years writing on my own without any recognition. You know, I started writing in 1945. In 1955 I published a book of my own with a vanity publisher, my first book, *Ommateum*. It wasn't until 1964 that I had a book accepted by Ohio State University Press, *Expressions of Sea Level*.

And the quality of that work, when looked at now—

Well, it's the best I have. It still sustains my reputation.

So you found it possible to be a poet, and to thrive as a poet, without the material trappings of celebration and success.

I couldn't avoid being a poet. I was really having a pretty rough time of things, and I had a lot of energy, and poems were practically the only recourse I had to alleviate that energy and that anxiety. I take no credit for all the poems I've written. They were a way of releasing anxiety.

When you say you were having a rough time, do you mean financially?

I had really no clearcut direction to my life for those years. I was working in business, not necessarily getting anywhere. It was just a lack of definition and direction. Financially, I didn't have a great deal of money, but I wasn't impoverished at that time.

You grew up impoverished in North Carolina.

We grew up rather poor, yes. But we didn't think of ourselves as poor. You've heard this said many times, I'm sure, about people in the Depression. We had a farm. It had been created as a sustenance farm, that is, you grew as many things as you might possibly need. My two sisters and I—I had two brothers but they died young—were never hungry. We always had clothes to wear. There was no money, however, in the South. I mean, during the Depression, there were actually no coins. People bartered. We had no money, so we were poor in that sense, but my family, in Southern terms, was fairly distinguished. My uncle was sheriff of the county for eight consecutive terms, longer than anyone had been. It was a highly prestigious job in those days and he was a splendid working man who was always erect and never carried a gun. He had a reputation for going into the most dangerous places unarmed and telling murderers or suspected murderers to come with him, and they would do it. He was also a considerable landowner in the county and owned what later became a whole beach down at the ocean, which was about forty miles from us. So he was a wealthy man and a highly prestigious man. I honored him greatly as a child. He sometimes helped us in the winters when we were broke.

So I was caught in the contradiction of feeling that I came from a good line and yet being inhibited as far as resources went. Since I was the only surviving Ammons of an enormous family, I was frequently told I was going to inherit forests and farms and things like that. But I didn't. By the time my uncle passed away I had left that region and never went back.

Sometimes it seems that the economic circumstances of one's childhood do play a determining role in one's psychological makeup later on. You can never really transcend those early insecurities.

I agree. Though there were other insecurities in my youth: the death of the two brothers, for example.

Were they younger brothers?

Yes. I was four when the brother eighteen months old died. I still carry images of that whole thing. And then the last member of our family was born dead. So I was the only son left.

Did you like working on the farm?

I hated it. You had to work in all kinds of weather. In the winter, you were in the swamp cutting trees for the fuel you needed in the summer for curing the tobacco. I mean it was just a constant round of hard work without reward because we remained in debt year after year after year.

Did you read books at home?

That came later. The only book I can remember having in the house apart from textbooks was the first eleven pages of *Robinson Crusoe*. I read that so many times I practically had it by memory. I don't know where the eleven pages came from, but there they were. Otherwise we read the Bible in Sunday school and we sang hymns. That was my exposure to words. And by the way I think that hymns have had an enormous influence on what I've written because they're the words I first heard and memorized.

When did you start writing?

When I went to high school (which in those times included the eighth grade), I wrote an essay and the teacher praised it highly and told all our classes, even the senior classes, about it. So I began to get some encouragement pretty early on about writing.

What was the essay about?

We were asked to read articles in the *Reader's Digest* and then to write our own version of the substance. I wrote about a cow they were trying to breed that would be only about thirty inches high but would give vast amounts of milk. I must have done this in an excellent style because as you can see the subject matter is not all that thrilling.

You mentioned Sunday school hymns as an important influence. I can see that in your very first poems, your "I am Ezra" poems. And certainly the religious impulse—the resolve to render the sacred in terms of the secular, to wed the lowly and the divine—is in much of your work. In a poem as recent as "The Damned" a mountaineer surrounded by silent peaks looks down from the summit and supposes that "these damned came of being / near the sanctified, wherever one finds / one one finds the other." Were you brought up to be serious about religion?

My mother was Methodist, but there was no Methodist church in our rural community, so I never went to a Methodist service. My father was Baptist. The New Hope Baptist Church was two miles away next to the elementary school. Nearer to us, less than a mile away, was the Spring Branch Fire-Baptized Pentecostal Church. I went to Sunday school there and the family sometimes attended preaching on Sundays, prayer meetings on Wednesday nights, or occasional weekly revivals. Once a two-week course in reading music was offered there— the do-re-me-so method—and I attended that when I was about eleven or twelve. As for the Baptist church, I went there for the Christmas Eve celebrations. For some reason, a paper bag containing an orange and apple, raisins, and a few English walnuts or pecans was always under the tree for me. The funerals in my family took place at the Baptist church. My little brothers, my grandmother, my aunts and uncles, and my father and mother were buried there. The Baptist church represented a higher social and intellectual class than did the Pentecostal. I identify coldly with the family religion. I take my religious spirit, whatever that is, from the Fire-Baptized Pentecostal.

Reading your poems I sometimes feel that they employ scientific means to reach a kind of religious end. I suppose I've always taken it for granted that you stopped going to church and that at some point— perhaps in your days as a sonar man (or "ping jockey") in the navy during World War II—poetry became the means by which you expressed your religious convictions.

One day when I was nineteen, I was sitting on the bow of the ship anchored in a bay in the South Pacific. As I looked at the land, heard the roosters crowing, saw the thatched huts, etc., I thought down to the water level and then to the immediately changed and strange world below the waterline. But it was the line inscribed across the variable land mass, determining where people would or would not live, where palm trees would or could not grow, that hypnotized me. The whole world changed as a result of an interior illumination: the water level was not what it was because of a single command by a higher power but because of an average result of a host of actions—runoff, wind currents, melting glaciers. I began to apprehend things in the dynamics of themselves—motions and bodies—the full account of how we came to be still a mystery with still plenty of room for religion, though, in my case, a religion of what we don't yet know rather than what we are certain of. I was de-denominated.

When did you join the navy?

I think it was '44. I came out in '46. I was in for nineteen months, about twelve of them in the South Pacific on a destroyer escort. It was on board this ship that I found an anthology of poetry in paperback. And I began to imitate those poems then and I wrote from then on.

Did you write about home and America and North Carolina or about what was happening in the South Pacific?

Mostly about what was happening in the South Pacific, including some humorous poems about the other members of the crew.

What has happened to these poems?

Oh, they're around.

Did you continue writing poems in civilian life?

I had never stopped writing but after having gotten a degree, the B.S. in general science, I borrowed the money to go back for a summer of education courses and then taught the first year as the principal of a three-teacher school in Cape Hatteras. That was 1949–50. That same fall, 1949, I got married. My wife Phyllis had been to Berkeley and liked it. So after a year of teaching, we went to Berkeley for two years. And there I did a good many English courses, completing the undergraduate degree. I had minored in English at Wake Forest so I completed that degree and did almost all the work toward a master's. And then we left and came back to South Jersey. I lived there for twelve years before coming here to Ithaca.

I know that you worked in your father-in-law's biological glass factory during that time. What did you do?

I was a vice president and in charge of sales. I did some administration and a lot of traveling to try to increase the business, which I did. We tripled the sales, and it became quite a successful company.

Were you interested in the work or was it dull?

It wasn't dull. I have a poem somewhere explaining how running a business is like writing a poem. In business, for example, you bring in the raw materials and then subject them to a certain kind of human change. You introduce the raw materials into a system of order, like the making of a poem, and once the matter is shaped it's ready to be shipped. I mean, the incoming and outgoing energies have achieved a kind of balance. Believe it or not, I felt completely confident in the work I was doing. And did it, I think, well.

That raises an interesting question. Most American poets work in universities and many if not most were trained in creative writing programs. It's the rare exception who makes his or her living outside the academy, as you did. And I'm not entirely convinced that this dependence is a healthy state of affairs.

Me neither. In my own case, working in industry wasn't exhausting—I mean poetically exhausting. I could write all the time. It's been true for me, in the thirty years I've been teaching, that as soon as the semester starts, my writing is done. The time I do any writing is Christmas vacation. That's when I wrote "Hibernaculum" and *Tape* and the "Essay on Poetics." Most of the things have been done between semesters or during the summers.

When were you invited to teach at Cornell?

I received an invitation from David Ray to give a reading here. He'd seen poems of mine in the *Hudson Review*. Also, I had that same year relieved Denise Levertov for six months as poetry editor of the *Nation*. And I had, without knowing the man, accepted a poem by David Ray and published it. And I suppose as a kind of return gesture, he invited me to come give a reading for $50 at Cornell and then he saw my poems in the *Hudson Review* and raised the fee to $150. So I came in July of 1963 and gave the reading and afterward [James] McConkey and [Baxter] Hathaway and others asked me if I would be interested in teaching. And though I was not a teacher and had not taught, I said yes because my wife and I were ready to make a move, and so we came to Cornell.

And you've been here ever since.

They were very good to me. At first I was the only non-Ph.D. in the [English] department, and they welcomed me and kept me. They gave me tenure. I thought it was quite remarkable.

Your standing-room-only poetry reading in Ithaca last December was memorable. I never thought I'd see you in a tuxedo. Did the event change your feelings about poetry readings, or confirm them? You used to hate giving readings. Why do you suppose people go to readings anyway?

It's a great mystery. When you consider how boring and painful nearly all poetry readings are, it's a wonder anyone shows up. And, wisely, few people do. I think it's not a love of poetry readings that attracts those who do come but theatre: to see what the beast, possibly already heard of, looks like in person; to make a poetry-business connection that could prove useful; to see who else comes to poetry readings; to endure pain and purgation; to pass one's books or pamphlets on to the reader; to see the reader mess up, suffer, lose control, and to enjoy the remarkable refreshment of finding him no less human, vulnerable or fallible, than oneself.

It may be time for another official Paris Review *interview question: what advice do you give to young writers?*

First of all, I omit praising them too much if I think that will be the catalyst that causes them to move into a seizure with a poetic way of life. Because I know how difficult that can be, and I tend to agree with Rilke that if it's possible for you to live some other life, by all means do so. If it seems to me that the person can't live otherwise than as a writer of poetry, then I encourage her to go ahead and do it. However the advice splits, depending on how I feel about the person. If I think he's really a genuine poet, I'd like to encourage him to get out into the so-called real world. If he seems like a poet who's going to get by through a kind of pressure of having to turn in so many poems per week in order to get a good grade or having to publish a book of poems in order to get promoted, then I encourage him to go to an M.F.A. program somewhere and become a so-called professional poet. You get to know people who know how to publish books, you begin to advance your career. I don't think that has very much to do with *real* poetry. It sometimes happens that these professional M.F.A. people are also poets; but it *rarely* happens.

You once said that trying to make a living from poetry is like putting chairs on butterfly wings.

Right. I'd stand by that.

How do you feel about government support of the arts?

I detest it. I detest it on many grounds, but three first. And the first is that the government gouges money from people who may need it for other purposes. Second, the money forced from needy average citizens is then filtered through the sieve of a bureaucracy which absorbs much of the money into itself and distributes the rest incompetently—since how could you expect the level of knowledge and judgment among such a cluster to be much in advance of the times? At the same time the government attaches strings to the money, not theirs in the first place, to those who gave it in the first place. And third, I detest the averaging down of expectation and dedication that occurs when thousands of poets are given money in what is really waste and welfare, not art at all. Artists should be left alone to paint or not to paint, write or not to write. As it is, the world is full of trash. The genuine is lost, and the whole field wallops with political and social distortions.

Do you feel the same way about private support of the arts?

Not at all. Everybody who loves the arts should have the liberty to sustain the particular arts he loves, whenever, wherever. If the love and money go to the popular arts, that's the way it should be. If there is an outcry for symphonic performances of the great B's, then that is what should be addressed. High arts that hang on almost vestigial in a culture should be addressed in their own scope, and I think they would not perish but that genius and energy would burst out whenever it's not already stifled by some blank, some holding grant, some template that just keeps blocking itself out.

Working with you on The Best American Poetry 1994, *I've noticed that you're not exactly overjoyed at the sight of poems that have a political agenda.*

It's not because I don't take political and large cultural matters very seriously. There are wrongs to be addressed. There are balances to be restored. The pragmatic merely supports my theoretical position. That is, what good does it do to write a poem almost no one reads about a matter of urgent interest? In a thousand years, if it is a magnificent, not half-baked poem, enough people will have read the poem to make a difference, but by then, where are the people, what is the issue? A letter to the editor of a newspaper or magazine could be read by 25,000 or 25,000,000 people. It would seem patently a waste of time not to try the letter.

A more general position has to do with autonomy. One does not want a poem to *serve* anything; the liberating god of poetry does not endorse servitude. What we want to see a poem do is to become itself, to reach as nearly a perfect state of self-direction and self-responsibility as can be believably represented. We want that for people too.

Your short poems are lyric outbursts and you've said that they come forth all at once. I know that you write your long poems in increments or passages. These seem in some ways deliberately imperfect—casual, expansive, all-inclusive, loose—in contrast to the shorter lyrics, which are all intensity and compression. Do your long poems entail a different process of writing?

Very different. In the long poem, if there is a single governing image at the center, then anything can fit around it, meanwhile allowing for a lot of fragmentation and discontinuity on the periphery. Short poems, for me, are coherences, single instances on the periphery of a nonspecified center. I revise short poems sometimes for years, whereas, since there is no getting lost in the long poem, I engage whatever comes up in the moment and link it with its moment.

What's your favorite among your long poems, if you have a favorite?

The poem that I like best, parts of the poem, is *The Snow Poems.* It seems to me in that poem I had a more ready availability to the names of things and to images of them than in any of the other long poems.

Tape for the Turn of The Year *had everything to do with the physical circumstances of its composition. You typed it on an adding machine tape, and this determined that you would have a poem of some length consisting of short lines and wide margins. I remember your telling me that the finished parts of the tape fell in coils in a wastepaper basket—kind of a forerunner of* Garbage. *Was this a way of reminding yourself not to take yourself too seriously?*

Yes. That's great. That's a good connection.

What started you going? How do you decide when to write a long poem like Tape *or* Garbage?

In 1963 when I did the *Tape* I had been thinking of having the primary motion of the poem down the page rather than across. The adding machine tape, less than two inches wide, seemed just right for a kind of breaking and spilling. Variations of emphasis and meaning which make the long horizontal line beautifully jagged and jerky became on the tape the left and right margins. Soon after I started the tape, I noticed resemblances between it and a novel. The point, like and unlike a novel, was to get to the other end; an arbitrary end would also be an "organic" end. The tape itself became the hero, beginning somewhere, taking on aspects and complications, coming to a kind of impasse, then finding some way to conclude. The material itself seemed secondary; it fulfilled its function whether it was good or bad material just by occupying space. In many ways the arbitrary was indistinguishable from the functional.

So with the other long poems, I wrote them when I had a new form to consider, some idea that would play through. *Garbage* came from the sight in passing of a great mound of garbage off the highway in Florida. When I found a single image that could sustain multiplicity, I usually could begin to write.

Were you surprised by the success enjoyed by Garbage? *The title is a pretty audacious gesture.*

I'd paid little attention to *Garbage* after writing it. But there was a real spurt of interest in the first five sections after they appeared in *APR* [*American Poetry Review*], so I engaged a student to type up the rest of it presentably, and I sent it off to Norton, where my editor surprisingly took it. My hope was to see the resemblances between the high and low of the secular and the sacred. The garbage heap of used-up language is thrown at the feet of poets, and it is their job to make or revamp a language that will fly again. We are brought low through sin and death and hope that religion can make us new. I used garbage as the material submitted to such possible transformations, and I wanted to play out the interrelationships of the high and the low. Mostly, I wanted something to do at the end of a semester.

How about Sphere: The Form of a Motion? *You once told me that the subtitle of that poem occurred to you at a Cornell faculty meeting when somebody talked about putting something in "the form of a motion" and you liberated this phrase from its parliamentary context.*

That's right. My application of the phrase had nothing to do with such meetings, but that was an interesting place for it to arise from. *Sphere* had the image of the whole earth, then for the first time seen on television, at its center. I guess it was about 1972. There was the orb. And it seemed to me the perfect image to put at the center of a reconciliation of One-Many forces. While I had had sort of philosophical formulations for the One-Many problem before, the earth seemed to be the actual body around which these forces could best be represented. So when I began *Sphere,* I knew what I wanted to do. I wanted to kind of complete that process, that marriage of the One-Many problem with the material earth.

The One-Many problem in philosophy has to do with the nature of reality, whether reality inheres in various things of which there is an infinite supply or whether there is one organizing, unifying principle that unites all the disparate phenomena. Is that a fair summation?

Yes. Another way that I think of it is the difference between focus and comprehensiveness. For example, if you wish to focus on a single point, or statement, to the extent you've purified the location or content of that statement, to that extent you would eliminate the comprehensiveness of things. You would have to leave out a great many things in order to focus on one thing. On the other hand, if you tried to include everything comprehensively, you would lose the focus. You see what I mean? So you have a polarity, a tension between bringing things into a sort of simplified clarity and going back to the wilderness of comprehensiveness, including everything.

Do you feel this as a tug of war inside yourself?

An ambivalence, I suppose. Or ambiguity. But somewhere along the line, I don't know just when, it seems to me I was able to manage the multifariousness of things and the unity of things so much more easily than I ever had before. I saw a continuous movement between the highest aspects of unity and the multiplicity of things, and it seemed to function so beautifully that I felt I could turn to any subject matter and know how to deal with it. I would know that there would be isolated facts and perceptions, that it would be possible to arrange them into propositions, and that these propositions could be included under a higher category of things—so that at some point there might be an almost contentless unity at the top of that sort of hierarchy. I feel that you don't have to know everything to be a master of knowing but you learn these procedures and then you can turn them toward any subject matter and they come out about the same. I don't know when I saw for myself the mechanism of how it worked for me. Perhaps it was when I stopped using the word *salient* so much and began to use the word *suasion*.

In a few weeks I'm going to be on a panel, a symposium on the question of "What is American about American poetry?" It seems like a good question although not an easy one. How should I answer?

Well, I think that question addresses itself to the past and not to the present or the future.

Do you think poetry has any future?

It has as much future as past—very little.

Could you elaborate on that?

Poetry is everlasting. It is not going away. But it has never occupied a sizable portion of the world's business and probably never will.

It seems that few of your contemporaries strike you as indispensable with the exception of Ashbery.

Wouldn't that be true of almost any period? Of the great many who write at any time, history has kept track of few.

Who are the few that you hold dearest?

Do I have to answer that? As a peripheral figure myself, I hestitate to comment on the devices of my contemporaries.

I meant from earlier generations.

I would say Chaucer, Spenser, Shakespeare, Milton. I'm not that crazy about Dryden and Pope and the eighteenth century, but I like the Romantics and I like Whitman and Dickinson. That's all. That's enough. Isn't it?

You've said many times that Ashbery is our greatest poet.

Ashbery has changed things for poetry in interesting ways above any other of my contemporaries. I admire almost everyone else equally.

You are often identified as a distinctively American poet.

Do you find that to be true?

Certainly your idiom is American, your conception of the poem, and I would say your relation to poetic tradition seems to me American.

I have tried to get rid of the Western tradition as much as possible. You notice I don't mention anything in my poetry having to do with Europe or where we come from. I never allude to persons or places or events in history. I really do want to begin with a bare space with streams and rocks and trees. I have a little, a tiny poem that says something about the only way you can do anything at all about all of Western culture is to fail to refer to it. And that's what I do. This makes my poetry seem, and maybe it actually is, too extremely non-cultural. And perhaps so. I grew up as a farmer and I had at one time a great love for the land because my life and my family and the people around me depended on weather and seasons and farming and seeds and things like that. So my love for this country was and is unlimited. But that's different from a governmental assessment of things, which I belive is basically urban. And it seems to me a poet such as Ashbery who locates himself in the city, which is the dominant culture now, is more representative of the American poet than perhaps I am.

You said you wanted to eliminate Western culture from your poetry. Why?

Well, I sort of disagree with it.

With the Cartesian mind, or with what? The philosophical tradition of the West? The Roman sense of justice?

If I get back to the pre-Socratics, I feel that I'm in the kind of world that I would enjoy to be in, but nothing since then. Especially in the last two thousand years, dominated by Christianity and the Catholic church and other religious organizations. I feel more nearly myself aligned with Oriental culture.

I've always been curious about why you've traveled so little. I think you spent a year in Italy.

Three months. We had the traveling fellowship of the American Academy, which was for a year, but we came back after three months. I lost twenty pounds and I couldn't wait to get home.

You didn't care for the experience of being an expatriate?

I hated it. I'm not interested in all that cultural crap. It was just a waste of time for me.

Maybe this is part of what you were talking about before when you spoke of your rejection of Western culture, by which I take it you mean more specifically a rejection of Europe or of European cultural domination.

Yes.

But it occurred to me that one reason you have traveled very little is—

There's no place to go.

There's no place to go?

Yeah, that's a good reason not to travel. Well, I'm interested in the Orient, but I'm really not interested in going there. I'm *not* interested in Europe. I have no interest whatsoever in going there. Every now and then I go to Owego and sometimes I go to Syracuse, sometimes to Geneva, Binghampton—all over the place.

Geneva, New York, rather than Geneva, Switzerland.

Geneva, New York, right.

It occurred to me that another reason might be that you'd already done a considerable journey in going from your origins on the coastal plain of North Carolina to the hills and lakes of central New York State. A critic could spin a parable about the northward progression of your life: from a state that was part of the Confederacy to a university town in—

In the Emersonian tradition. [Laughs] In fact there *is* an essay about how I came to the North and took over the Emersonian tradition.

I thought you had decided to become influenced by Emerson only after Bloom told you that you'd been.

That's basically correct, except that I did have a course on Emerson and Thoreau at Wake Forest. The professor was basically a preacher, however, who treated the hour as an occasion for sermonizing. But yes—it's a marriage of the South to the North.

What is?

The movement of my life.

You've spent more time in the North.

Much more. I lived my first twenty-four years in the South. I've been in Ithaca for thirty years.

Are you conscious of being a Southerner here?

I don't hear my own voice but of course everyone else does and I'm sure they're all conscious of the fact that I'm Southern but I am mostly not conscious of it. In the first years, I was tremendously nostalgic, constantly longing for the South: for one's life, for one's origin, for one's kindred. Now I feel more at home here than I would in the South. But I don't feel at home—I'll never feel at home—anywhere.

III.

Poems and Comment

Inside Out

Among the many kinds of poetic form are those that realize themselves in stasis (achieved by motion) and those that identify their shape, their intelligibility through motion, as motion. Sonnets, villanelles are inventions like triangles (these may be discoveries) and their use is to cause "nature" to find its form only if it can do so in arbitrary human terms. There is the famous possibility that internal, organic form and imposed external form may on splendid occasions complement each other as in a single necessity. But arbitrary forms please us even when they are interposed and impositional because they reassure us that we can repress nature, our own natures, and achieve sufficient expression with no more than trifling threat, or we can take delight that we, mere human beings, have devised systems nature (or energy) is clearly, truly, abundantly released through. The danger is that arbitrary forms may be boringly clever compensations for a lack of native force, boxes to be filled with crushed material, boxes which may be taken to exhaust the unlimited existences inventive prosody can find to station the arbitrary in the work of art.

There are gestural and figural forms, too, internal assimilations that are narratives shaping transactions. I've chosen a short poem of mine to show how the figure of winding can suggest the manifold accuracy by which a brook or stream summarizes the meteorological action of whole terrains, so

"Inside Out" first appeared in *Epoch* 33, no. 1 (1983): 38–39. Reprinted in *Ecstatic Occasions, Expedient Forms,* ed. David Lehman (New York: Collier Books, 1987).

that wherever there are hills and valleys one can confidently look to find the winding of this dragon of assimilation.

Serpent Country

Rolled off a side of mountains or
hills, bottomed
out in flatland but getting

away, winding,
will be found a
bright snake—brook, stream, or river, or,

in sparest gatherings,
a wash of stones or a green
streak of chaparral across sand.

The figures, though, in this poem are controlled by other progressions, and these progressions are the real form of the poem. In one motion, the figure enlarges from brook to stream to river, but then the figure disappears till the only "stream" in the landscape is a trace of green in the brush where an underground stream once briefly moved. The form of the poem is the motion from the indelible river to the nearly vanished green. It is a figure of disappearing. That is one kind of internal form. It allows to nature full presence and action, it excludes nothing a priori and imposes nothing. It discovers within. It uses human faculties to imagine means, analogies to simplify so much material, to derive from the broad sweep of action the accurate figure and the ineluctable, suitable form of motion.

Motion Which Disestablishes
Organizes Everything

William James (*The Varieties of Religious Experience,* p. 84) is
    to be
commended for penning out of our finest recommendations
    for the bright outlook:

he was so miserable himself he knew how to put a fine
    point on the exact
prescription: he knew that anybody who knows anything
    about human

existence knows it can be heavy: in fact, it can be so
    heavy it can undo
its own heaviness, the knees can crumple, the breath
    and heart beat,

not to mention the bowels, can become irregular, etc.: but
    the world,
William knew, sardonic and skeptical, can characterize
    sufferers of such

symptoms malingering wimps, a heaviness not to be
    welcomed by a person who
like me feels like one of those: weight begets weight and
    nature works as well

"Motion Which Disestablishes Organizes Everything" originally ap-
peared in *The Hudson Review* (Summer 1987) and was reprinted in
The Best American Poetry 1988, ed. John Ashbery; series ed. David
Lehman (New York: Scribners, 1988).

(and mindlessly) down as up: you have to put English of
    your own into
the act misleading the way into lightenings: brightness,
    however

desirable, is a losing battle, though, and James knew it can
    be depended on
more often than not that folks won't have spare
    brightnesses on them every

morning that they want your heaviness to cost them: so, in
    general, if
someone asks how you are, no matter how you are, say
    something nice: say,

"fine," or "marvelous morning," and, this way, hell
    gradually notches up
toward paradise, a misconstruction many conspire to
    forward because

nearly all, maybe all, prefer one to the other: oppositions
    make things costly:
crooked teeth encourage the symmetry of braces but as
    soon as everybody's

teeth are perfect, crooked teeth misalign: something is
    always working
the other way: if you let the other way go, you get more in
    Dutch for

while the other way at first may constitute an alternative
    mainstream,
pretty soon it breaks up into dispersive tributaries and
    splinters a

rondure of fine points into branches and brooklets till it
    becomes
impossible to get a hold on it, a river system running
    backwards:

be bright: that is a wish that can be stable: you can always
    think of
happiness because it's wished right out of any rubbings
    with reality, so

you can keep the picture pure and steady: I always imagine
   a hillock,
about as much as I can get up these days, with a lovely
   shade tree and under

the tree this beautiful girl, unnervingly young, who
   projects golden
worlds: this scene attracts me so much that even though
   I'm a little

scared by it it feels enlivening, a rosy, sweet enlivening:
   poets
can always prevent our hubris, reminding us how the
   coffin slats peel

cloth and crack in, how the onset of time strikes at birth,
   how love falters,
how past the past is, how the eyes of hungry children feed
   the flies.

On "Motion Which Disestablishes
Organizes Everything"

When poems get too skinny and bony, emaciated nearly into left-hand margin, so highly articulated their syllables crystallize, I go back to long lines to loosen up, to blur the issues of motion into minor forms within larger motions. I believe something like that was taking place some three or four years ago when I wrote this poem and three or four others like it.

"On 'Motion Which Disestablishes Organizes Everything' " appeared in *The Best American Poetry 1988*, ed. John Ashbery; series ed. David Lehman (New York: Scribners, 1988).

Making Change

The deeps the agencies of money spring from are as mystical, as unavailable to analysis and definition, as are those of poetry, and the surface operations of both money and poetry spell out into such vast systems of differentiation and similitude, that I feel excused, in a short piece, to confine my attention to a single thread or axis through these complexes; I mean, the transformative agency of these two.

Societies formed or founded on altruistic or utopian fictions (poetic fictions) often prove temporary, and not just societies, but causes coming out of pure good and tending toward pure good seem often shallow, unworkable, or forced, and are almost always in deficit, and in need of pure contribution. There is little transforming in such systems: the good is made good or better. A reality underlying altruism is made clear in a recent poem of mine:

> *Resolve*
>
> We must work
> in the spirit
> of unity and
> cooperation; I'll supply
> the unity and
> you supply the
> cooperation.

Nonimpositional liveliness comes from the so-called negative emotions. Societies in which the members are allowed to devise

---

"Making Change" first appeared in *Epoch* 38, no. 2 (1989): 138–39.

systems answering to greed, competition, fury, repression, egotism are generally fully energized. The agencies of money answer and enable the tendencies of "negative" feelings so as to provide transformative possibilities potentially and usually strengthening to the whole society, some imbalance and exploitation unavoidable, of course, but correctable.

Poetry, I think, plays a similar role, moving the feelings of marginality, of frustration, of envy, hatred, anger into verbal representations that are formal, structuring, sharable, revealing, releasing, social, artful. These negative situations, truly and appropriately represented, alert our sympathies for and knowledge of misfortune and terrible isolation so that we can act individually toward real situations and real people, where the rhetoric of altruism is nearly mindless automatism.

Money, like poetry, though inexhaustibly entertainable and entertaining, has its limitations, of course. Where there is little money, there is unrealistic expectation. Money is direly sweet where it is needed and a boring abundance where it is not needed. Poetry dances in neglect, waste, terror, hopelessness— wherever it is hard to come by. But too much poetry, or what passes for poetry, sickens the stomach. In the reconciliations of opposite states, in the uninhibited negotiations between states that money and poetry facilitate, we have cultural systems that give nothing up as negative and that transform what is negative into useful and meaningful parlances.

Anxiety's Prosody

Anxiety clears meat chunks out of the stew, carrots, takes
the skimmer to floats of greasy globules and with cheesecloth

filters the broth, looking for the transparent, the colorless
essential, the unbeginning and unending of consommé: the

open anxiety breezes through thick conceits, surface congestions
(it likes metaphors deep-lying, out of sight, their airs misting

up into, lighting up consciousness, unidentifiable presences),
it distills consonance and assonance, glottal thickets, brush

clusters, it thins the rhythms, rushing into longish gaits, more
distance in less material time: it hates clots, its stump-fires

level fields: patience and calm define borders and boundaries,
hedgerows, and sharp whirls: anxiety burns instrumentation

matterless, assimilates music into motion, sketches the high
suasive turnings, mild natures tangled still in knotted clumps.

"Anxiety's Prosody" originally appeared in *Poetry* (© October 1988)
by the Modern Poetry Association and was reprinted in *The Best
American Poetry 1989,* ed. Donald Hall; series ed. David Lehman
(New York: Scribners, 1989). Reprinted with permission of the Edi-
tor of *Poetry.*

On "Anxiety's Prosody"

I remember reading somewhere—in Shakespeare, maybe—that a person under extreme anxiety tears off his or her clothes. In a state of anxiety you can't stand corporality and you want to attenuate into openness and strip away the bodily impediments. That relieves the anxiety in some way. Anxiety tries to get rid of everything thick and material—to arrive at a spiritual emptiness, the emptiness that is spiritual.

"On 'Anxiety's Prosody' " appeared in *The Best American Poetry 1989*, ed. Donald Hall; series ed. David Lehman (New York: Scribners, 1989).

The Damned

This fellow grazed his woolly goats
on a high ledge, a very high place
snowless in summer, but it was,

perhaps because of the fellow's loneliness,
a region in which the mountains talked,
it seemed, and over a miles-wide gulf,

summits forever white rose useless
in august assumptions the polish of
the wind and glare of the sun sanctified,

the fellow supposed, and he thought,
well, few know that kind of thing,
a rare condition, though not good for grass:

and the fellow, noting that the peaks
had really said nothing yet, went to
the ledge-edge and looked down on the

summits of sweet-green hills
and runoff rills so lowly and supposed,
again, that these damned came of being

near the sanctified, wherever one finds
one one finds the other, and he wondered
if the heights knew, somehow, that the energy

of their complacency came of
a differentiation imposed on the backs,
so to speak, of the lowly, and he

"The Damned" originally appeared in *The Yale Review* (June 1988) and was reprinted in *The Best American Poetry 1990,* ed. Jorie Graham; series ed. David Lehman (New York: Scribners, 1990).

wondered if the sanctified would not
wish to remove themselves, somehow, if
they knew that, but then, he supposed,

knowing that would spoil the sanctification
anyhow, so maybe the peaks could shine
there, since it seemed they had to, as

wastelands of what it means to be way high:
but the mountains had said nothing and
the fellow supposed himself a supposition,

too, no one having agreed with him, the peaks
too taken aback, except for this longing
for the valleys roaring in his guts.

On "The Damned"

The writing of nature poetry is considered a pretty jaded activity in our time, a holdover or negative from the nine-teenth century. Even so, I'm sure there were and are many kinds of nature poetry, and I hang on to one variable kind typical of my work throughout my writing life. My kind may not be mine alone—others may use the same stance—but I haven't studied others; I've merely tried to know my own way.

It seems obvious to me that things and the world came first. In spite of all philosophical sophistry and negativism and sub-jectivism, I believe what's "written" in the rocks. I believe that this planet is ancient, that it preceded man or manlike crea-tures by billions of years and preceded words and languages by at least an equal time. The center of consciousness for me is not verbal. I live in a world of things, not texts, not written texts. I feel that languages are arbitrary systems of intrinsic coherence and incoherence that arise, change, and disappear in response to circumstance, taking nothing from and adding nothing to nature. Our minds, the "minds" of our predecessors, whether verbal, impressionistic, instinctive, or hormonal rose out of the creative forces of nature itself. Nature produced us. We were here with formed spines and backbones, with complex arterial systems, with enzymes and electrical charges long before we had names for any of it.

So I feel deeply conditioned by nature. I expect to find, when I look at things around me, the sources of myself. But I

"On 'The Damned' " appeared in *The Best American Poetry 1990*, ed. Jorie Graham; series ed. David Lehman (New York: Scribners, 1990).

don't go to nature for "sermons in brooks" or for cute mes
sages from rocks and weeds. Nature is not verbal. It is there. It
comes first. I have found, though, that at times when I have
felt charged with a vague energy or when I have moved into
an intense consideration of what it means to be here, I some-
times by accident "see" a structure or relationship in nature
that clarifies the energy, releases it. Things are visible ideas. I
recognize a correspondence, partial, of course, between my
considerations and some configuration of things.

In "The Damned," based, I imagine, on some photo of the
Himalayan peaks, I found engaged my worry about what
might be called "innocent guilt," something akin to but proba-
bly not the same thread as original sin. In the hierarchy of
peaks the sainted summits, let's say, are not in spite of their
height and purity innocent of the damnation of the lesser
peaks, those that lack the majesty of thin air. We, as people,
cannot be disentangled from the network of humanity, even
though we have not intended to rise at the expense of others,
and we are not free of an obligation to others, even if others
are incapable of adding anything to us. I won't play out the
disposition of the whole poem into exposition, except to note
my dissatisfaction with the last line, which seems to me vulgar
in its strong play. A quieter line is needed. And to say that the
lower summits may have compensations of their own power-
ful enough to cast the highest summits as the damned.

I don't say that nature gives me a complete text—or any
textual analogy. But there are often configurations of things
that surprisingly relate to and often clarify adumbrations we
are daily swaying with.

On *Garbage*

I wrote *Garbage* in the late spring of 1989. Because of some medical problems that developed soon after the poem was written, I didn't send it anywhere for a long time. The *American Poetry Review* very generously accepted it but because of a backlog had to delay publication for a while. By Capote's view, the poem is typing, not writing. I wrote it for my own distraction, improvisationally: I used a wide roll of adding machine tape and tore off the sections in lengths of a foot or more. The whole poem is over eighty pages long, so I sent only the first five sections to *APR.* Norton published the whole poem as a book in 1993. I've gone over and over my shorter poems to try to get them right, but alternating with work on short poems, I have since the sixties also tried to get some kind of rightness into improvisations. The arrogance implied by getting something right the first time is incredible, but no matter how much an ice-skater practices, when she hits the ice it's all a one-time event: there are falls, of course, but when it's right, it seems to have been right itself.

"On *Garbage*" appeared in *The Best American Poetry 1993*, ed. Louise Glück; series ed. David Lehman (New York: Scribner's, 1993).

UNDER DISCUSSION
David Lehman, General Editor
Donald Hall, Founding Editor

Volumes in the Under Discussion series collect reviews and essays about individual poets. The series is concerned with contemporary American and English poets about whom the consensus has not yet been formed and the final vote has not been taken. Titles in the series include: